PRAISE FOR *HOW WOULD JESUS VOTE?*

"Darrell Bock, one of the most respected biblical scholars alive, offers gospel-informed counsel on overcoming the gridlock we see all around us. In an era of cable TV shouting matches and social media wars, we should listen to this wisdom."

—Russell Moore, president of the Ethics & Religious
Liberty Commission, Southern Baptist Convention

"Dr. Bock does not simply call us to think outside the box, but to think outside our bias—to rethink what we believe and why, to engage in genuine dialogue with mutual respect, and to work toward a greater common good for both believer and unbeliever like."

—Chip Ingram, teaching pastor of Living on the Edge
and author of *Culture Shock*

"I am totally undone by this book! It is challenging, engaging, and convicting. When I served in government, my thinking was political—it was far from concern for human flourishing and common good. Who considers that in today's political environment? No one. This book calls us all to reflect on our political thinking in light of biblical values. *How Would Jesus Vote?* is the blueprint for those who want to see serious change in this country, from politicians to those who influence them. This is an excellent work!"

—Dorothy Burton, president and CEO of Christians in Public
Service, Inc., and former chief of staff to the Dallas County Judge

"We've had more than enough focus on the things that drive us apart. Darrell Bock offers a thoughtful and biblically grounded summary of the principles and practices that can bring Christians together—with each other and also with their unbelieving neighbors. He doesn't try to lay down the one right answer to each issue. Instead, he shows that, while there are hard choices and we will often disagree, there is a broad social consensus defined by stewardship, goodwill, and accountability, within which we can have our debates as fellow citizens who love each other. If you don't know how Jesus would vote, you'll want to read this book; if you think you do know how Jesus would vote, you definitely need to read this book!"

—Greg Forster, director of the Oikonomia Network,
Trinity International University

"The ethical question 'What would Jesus do?' now becomes 'What does Jesus want *me* to do, here and now, in the complex modern world in which I live?' Thankfully, the Bible provides real guidance in answering this question. Yet little of that guidance comes from simple proof texts; rather, it comes through the sort of biblical engagement Darrell Bock offers in this book. Bock does not aim to give quick answers to every question—not possible!—but he does provide a model for wrestling with the issues in the light of God's Word—a model that Christians will increasingly need in the years ahead. This is a much-needed attempt to think 'Christianly' about the moral and political dilemmas of our day."

—Duane Litfin, president emeritus, Wheaton College

"Navigating the radically altered American culture in a way that is consistent with Scripture and honoring to Christ is a major challenge. Like wanderers in the darkest of nights, we long for someone to shed light on our puzzling journey. Thankfully,

Darrell Bock has brought the light of Scripture to help us find our way. This is a must-read for any of us who desire to be effective for Christ in an increasingly hostile environment."

—Joseph Stowell, president, Cornerstone University

"*How Would Jesus Vote?* is a bold book that refuses to consign our faith in a living God to a privatized piety. As a refreshing alternative, Darrell Bock encourages us with a vision for a Christian political engagement that would be a blessing to all of our neighbors. Bock's faithful engagement of some of the most complex, fraught issues of our time offers a path from endless political gridlock to seeking the peace and prosperity of the nation and communities where God has planted us. Oh, that we would grab hold of this vision and let it guide us in the days ahead! I recommend this book for all who want to honor God in their whole lives, including their politics."

—Michael Wear, founder of Public Square Strategies LLC
and former White House Staff

"In *How Would Jesus Vote?* Bock calls for a calm, reasoned conversation regarding 'hot-button' issues, based on two essential foundations of the United States government—reason and humble faith. Bock challenges a number of the sacred cows of modern conservative thought without abandoning a truly conservative and thoroughly biblical approach. On issue after issue—including immigration, sexuality, health care, gun control, and even the size of government—Dr. Bock challenges readers to engage vigorously but respectfully, keeping to the issues and avoiding personal attack. His call for a balance of conviction and compromise is one Christ-followers of every political persuasion would do well to heed, and one designed to

move us toward that ideal advocated by our founding fathers—
the common good."

—Don Hawkins, DMin, former president of Southeastern
Bible College, president of Encouragement Communications,
and director, The Worship Channel

"The best professors do not tell us what to think. They teach
us *how* to think and to think well. Dr. Darrell Bock is such an
instructor in the classroom and in life. His newest book, *How
Would Jesus Vote?*, combines biblical thinking with the scholar-
ship of a distinguished professor and precise thinker. If you aim
to represent Christ in your voting as well as your living, *How
Would Jesus Vote?* is an invaluable resource. If you are looking
for biblical thinking and sound reasoning to help you navigate
changing times and politics, I highly recommend Dr. Darrell
Bock as a trusted guide and biblical voice."

—John S. Dickerson, author of *The Great
Evangelical Recession* and *I Am Strong*

"Renowned New Testament scholar Darrell Bock presents his
biblical perspective on contemporary politics, encouraging
readers to approach it with humble faith. He engages a range
of complex issues in a manner that will promote biblical reflection and dialogue. This book offers an important reminder that
the ultimate goal of our political activity—like all aspects of our
lives—should be loving God and neighbor."

—Amy E. Black, professor of Political Science, Wheaton College

"In *How Would Jesus Vote?* biblical scholar Darrell Bock offers a
valuable discussion for thoughtful Christians of how holy scripture informs the values we bring to the public sphere. Often

drawing on the findings of current research in the natural and social sciences, Bock provides an attractive model of how we are to seriously follow Jesus' command to love our neighbor. As a Christian economist, I particularly find helpful Bock's presentation of the complexity of biblical teaching on wealth and poverty. He rightly identifies the goodness of material creation while highlighting the link between greed and idolatry and the dominant scriptural emphasis on the wise stewardship of our resources in caring for and empowering the poor. Without downplaying the importance of convictions, Bock seeks not to provide his readers with precise answers but to challenge them to inquire of themselves whether or not they are asking the right questions. He encourages us to employ grace and fairness in political discourse in the face of the limited knowledge we must each rely on as creatures in a fallen world. I strongly recommend this book for Christians interested in how to bring a reasoned, discerning and informed voice of mutual regard and accountability in dialogue with our neighbors who share the image of God with us."

—Edd Noell, professor of Economics and
Business, Westmont College

"At a time when Christians increasingly feel like strangers in a strange land, what is needed is a primer on how to engage difficult social matters in the public square. Darrell Bock reminds readers of the fundamental biblical principles and virtues that should inform Christian opinions on a wide range of pressing topics. This book is wisdom for constructive Christian civil discourse in a rapidly changing social landscape."

—M. Daniel Carroll-Rodas, Blanchard Professor of
Old Testament, Wheaton Graduate School and College

"Professor Darrell Bock's timely book covers all the major political issues and controversies of today. Dr. Bock acknowledges early in the book that he is a theologian, not a lawyer or legislator. Yet, he engages American culture as few do and models how all of us, lawyers, legislators, voters, and citizens of all stripes should be thinking and interacting with those with whom we disagree. Much of the discussion in Christian circles involves interpreting biblical texts through the eyes of political presuppositions rather than understanding the biblical text and applying it to the political dialogue. Dr. Bock's book is a corrective to this method of understanding the text, and encourages us to think 'Christianly' about the political issues that are at the center of so much public discourse today. For those who might not be part of a faith community, Dr. Bock provides a broader reflection that does not fit neatly on the conservative/liberal/progressive scale and yet provides the foundation for thoughtful dialogue that is sorely needed today."

—Hon. Rollin A. Van Broekhoven, JD, LLM, DPhil, DLitt, DPS, LLD; chancellor, Oxford Graduate School; visiting scholar, University of Oxford Centre for Socio-Legal Studies; fellow, American Friends of Oxford House; retired US federal judge

"This book encourages us to consider, or reconsider, the fundamental character of Christian witness in American culture today. It is well argued and has the potential to spark much-needed discussions and lively conversations. It could not be more timely."

—Michael Cromartie, vice president, Ethics and Public Policy Center in Washington DC

HOW WOULD JESUS VOTE?

DO YOUR POLITICAL POSITIONS *REALLY* ALIGN WITH THE BIBLE?

DARRELL L. BOCK

HOWARD BOOKS
An Imprint of Simon & Schuster, Inc.

NEW YORK   NASHVILLE   LONDON   TORONTO   SYDNEY   NEW DELHI

Howard Books
An Imprint of Simon & Schuster, Inc.
1230 Avenue of the Americas
New York, NY 10020

CONTENTS

Introduction: *Beyond Gridlock*   xiii

1. How It All Began: *The Principles That Built America*   1

2. Starting Points: *Loving Your Neighbor*   17

3. Starting Points: *Big Government or Small?*   27

4. Economics and Poverty: *Personal Wealth or Shared Resources?*   41

5. Health Care: *Comprehensive Coverage or Choice?*   59

6. Immigration: *The Character of a Society*   79

7. Gun Control: *Self-Defense or Restraint*   103

8. Foreign Policy and Globalization: *National Interest or Common Good?*   119

9. War and Peace: *"Just War" or Pacifism?*   133

10. Race: *Equality, Violence, and Justice*   151

11. Education: *Relating to a Globalized World*   163

12. The Family: *Sexuality and Individual Rights*   185

13. Abortion and Embryos: *Right to Life or
    Right to Choose?*   209

Conclusion: *Engagement, Respect, and Loving
Your Neighbor*   221

Notes   231

Aₘ...America's problem isn't too much religion, or too little of it. It's *bad* religion: the slow-motion collapse of traditional Christianity and the rise of a variety of destructive pseudo-Christianities in its place. . . . The secular mistake has been to assume that every theology tends inevitably toward the same follies and fanaticisms, and to imagine that a truly post-religious culture is even possible, let alone desirable. The religious mistake has been to fret over the threat posed by explicitly anti-Christian forces, while ignoring or minimizing the influence that the apostles of pseudo-Christianity exercise over the American soul. Along the way both sides [secular antagonists and religious conservatives] have embraced a wildly simplified vision of our culture in which the children of light contend with the children of darkness, and every inch of ground is claimed by absolute truth or despicable error.

—ROSS DOUTHAT, *NEW YORK TIMES* COLUMNIST, *BAD RELIGION: HOW WE BECAME A NATION OF HERETICS*

Beyond Gridlock

GRIDLOCK. WHEN I hear this word, I often think of traffic. Crawling along at escalator pace with 500,000 of my closest friends is the epitome of dysfunction. A car is designed to get us from A to B, but being stuck in traffic is the opposite of movement and progress.

Today the word *gridlock* brings something else to mind. It describes the dysfunction of our government. Polls tell us that people are discouraged with politicians' inability to govern well. It makes no difference if a Democrat or a Republican is in the White House. Heroes and villains simply change locations. Each side utilizes the same tactics to discredit the views of the other. Neither group sees merit on the other side of the table. Both sides think only morons or traitors would propose what they oppose. Little takes place. Nothing changes. Gridlock.[1]

Just as a car has a specific design—getting us from A to B—our government, too, is designed for a purpose: legislating how a diverse community can live together as neighbors. Yet our government has failed miserably in doing this. Watching the news, we see that our government is stuck, going almost nowhere. Everyone is frustrated, and each side always blames the other. Every group is engaged in a culture war for all the stakes. All stand for country and the flag. The opposition has nothing of value to offer. The result is an OK Corral–style standoff.

But might the fault be ours collectively?

Politicians on both sides of the aisle and religious leaders of all stripes invoke Jesus or the Bible to appeal to the Judeo-Christian roots of our culture. It is a way of arguing that God is on our side: There is nothing to discuss. My side is right. But life is complex and so are the ways Scripture and Jesus engage life.

Politicians on both sides of the aisle invoke Jesus or the Bible to appeal to the Judeo-Christian roots of our culture. It is a way of arguing that God is on our side.

This book is an attempt to present the values of Jesus and Scripture in a way that challenges cherry-picking on complex issues of policy. It's about biblical values, government, and our neighbors. We'll discuss questions such as: What did Jesus say about how we live well in a society as diverse as ours? What can and should we expect of our government? Why are politicians who proclaim Jesus and Judeo-Christian values so gridlocked? How can Bible-believing elected officials "love their neighbors" as they govern with nonbelievers? How do biblical and human values impact our pursuit of love, justice, power sharing, equality, prosperity, and peace? *Is there a way out of this gridlock?*

In our pursuit of answers to these questions, we'll also consider the history of the tensions that drive our discourse and the flaws in how we conduct this social and political discourse. Based both on the Bible and on reason, we'll make a case for the validity of virtue, spirituality, and religion as we approach our mutual, corporate task—pursuit of the common good in a diverse society. We'll look at the values—many of them biblical—that each side brings forward on an array of issues. We'll ask secularists to consider the impact of a valueless society or a society where everyone picks what is right in his or her eyes. We'll look at ways to avoid tribalism and seek approaches to working out our conflicting desires and claims—without vilifying those who think differently. We'll also take a hard look at a category many Christian and non-Christian thinkers believe is central to the conversation: the common good. We'll consider how to find and define it and what to do when people hold little in common and debate the definition of *good*.

Even though the book's title is *How Would Jesus Vote?* I need to make the point that we don't even know if Jesus *would* vote. His life on this earth did not explicitly intersect politics at all— except that he told his disciples to pay taxes. He did draw attention to all people's responsibility to the Creator God, a clear challenge to the idea that the emperor was a god, but little of what he said focused directly on Roman government. And I also need to make the point that I certainly don't presume to know how Jesus would vote if he did step into a voting booth. But we can know the principles he taught that relate to how we are to interact with others. If these principles were lived out when dividing issues were discussed, then we might be able to avoid the gridlock that has brought our nation's governing process to a standstill. It's what we can know from Scripture and from Jesus that we bring to this discussion in hopes of learning to love our neighbors throughout the political process. It is in this sense that we ask the question, How would Jesus vote?

This book begins with an introduction to the principles our country was founded on, then moves to two "Starting Points" chapters that lay the foundation we'll need before we begin talking about the issues that divide us. After this groundwork has been laid, the remaining chapters will examine some of the most contentious political topics of our time in the light of Scripture and the teachings of Jesus. Our end goal is not to land rigidly on a specific position, but to arrive at a different kind of conversation—a conversation where differences are heard and respect is shared. Living with and loving our neighbor means being able to disagree yet dialogue well. It means discovering a route out of gridlock and finding a way to govern more effectively in a world of conflicting ideas, flawed people, and competing ideologies.

If the possibility of another way intrigues you as it does me, then I invite you to keep reading.

HOW WOULD
JESUS VOTE?

O F ALL the dispositions and habits which lead to political prosperity, religion and morality are indispensable supports. In vain would that man claim the tribute of patriotism, who should labor to subvert these great pillars of human happiness, these firmest props of the duties of men and citizens. The mere politician, equally with the pious man, ought to respect and to cherish them.

—GEORGE WASHINGTON, FIRST PRESIDENT OF THE UNITED STATES, FAREWELL ADDRESS, SEPTEMBER 19, 1796

I

How It All Began

The Principles That Built America

Our Founding Father George Washington did what good fathers often do—he passed on fatherly words of wisdom to the children he cared for, our nation's citizens. As he refused a third term as president, George Washington gave a farewell address to his beloved country and urged them to continue on the path he had started them on.

REASON AND HUMBLE FAITH

The bulk of this book will deal with some of the most polarizing political issues that face our nation. But before we launch into that discussion, we must lay some essential groundwork. Michael Novak, in *On Two Wings*, documents how the Founding Fathers launched this nation into flight on two wings, *reason* and *humble faith*—a humble faith rooted in Judeo-Christian revelation.[1] Here, "humble faith" means a faith that believes and trusts in God, but also a faith that recognizes the value of others—as they may help me see things I have missed. Humble faith also means that I don't rely on my instincts, which can be selfish, but that I be open to challenge that pushes me toward a sense of duty to others.

Michael Novak shows, through a series of citations, that many of our Founding Fathers held to the concepts of reason and humble faith in one form or another. He argues persuasively that much of recent history has forgotten the wing of humble faith, leaving our understanding of history and ourselves out of balance. After all, who can fly with only one wing? This unbalanced approach focuses on the influence of the Enlightenment and reason while ignoring religion, or faith—thus marginalizing the role of religion and treating it as irrelevant. As Novak puts it, revelation and reason have been and can be allies. Religious concern, properly modulated, can help us gain balance in the contentious debates over how we treat one another.

But if religion, morality, and virtue inform how a people function together in a healthy way, how do we avoid the historical misuse of religion and the conflict it brings? It was this very misuse in Europe that led to the Thirty Years' War and the Hundred Years' War. The abuse of religion is the reason the pilgrims came to America to launch an important social experiment, namely setting up a state that lacked a state religion and that had religious liberty—a new idea for a new world.[2] Religious liberty was created with the intent of having not freedom *from* religion, but freedom *of* religion. The public square was meant to encourage reflection and even religious discourse. People were free to worship or not worship. It was a society that was designed to be diverse, function together, and yet pursue virtue and the common good.

Our founders included orthodox believers, like John Witherspoon, as well as Unitarians who did not believe in miracles, like Thomas Jefferson. An array of leaders, diverse in their beliefs, worked together to form a more perfect union and seek a public common good. This dissimilar group of leaders led to a diversity that worked—even though opposing beliefs were hotly debated. John Witherspoon and Thomas Jefferson were able to sit at a table and design a government that could work for each of them, as different as they were. Have we lost that ability? They preserved public space for each side and called that space religious liberty as part of a representative government with shared power and checks and balances. This preserved space juxtaposed those who believed in providence with those concerned about excessive religious influence. Both could make their case and negotiate in public space without threat of reprisal. Steven Smith called this working cohesion around religious liberty "the American Settlement." Both sides learned how to coexist and did so effectively until legal decisions of the 1950s and '60s broke the détente that had previously existed, leading us straight into the culture wars.[3]

Religious liberty was created with the intent of having not freedom *from* religion, but freedom *of* religion.

How did our Founding Fathers do it? In part, they were able to work together because they understood that a healthy society must not only elevate freedom but also pursue virtue, or moral excellence. They also understood that a state that tries to control a person's conscience pulls in the direction of tyranny and despotism. And they understood that divided power was the best kind of power and that it provided protection from abuse by the power people, and especially by a majority of people.

The essential components of *virtue, freedom, power,* and *conscience* live in tension with one another. Life is messy and so is governing the mixed bag of minds and souls that populate our world. In such a mix of views, how can we live well together? How can we heed Washington's advice that political prosperity requires religion and morality? How can we work together when we think so differently from our neighbor?

SCRIPTURE AND THE ORIGINS OF THE UNITED STATES

At the time our Constitution was written, the goal for government was relatively modest. It was written at a time of competing views across a spectrum—from orthodox Christians to deists, from those who held to states' rights to those who wanted centralized federal power. How could a nation function in such diversity? The goal was to form a "more perfect union." A failed Articles of Confederation led to a redo of the core document of the nation. Out of failure came a success.

The new document began with this sentence, "We the People of the United States, in order to form a more perfect Union, establish justice, insure domestic tranquility, provide for the common defense, promote the general welfare, and secure the blessings of liberty to ourselves and our posterity, do ordain and establish this Constitution for the United States of America." The Bill of Rights made it clear that the nation was not created to be a strict theocracy. Separation of church and state was a reaction against theocracy, an Enlightenment protection against the kind of religious war that had wracked Europe. Justice, peace, defense, general welfare, and the pursuit of liberty were the reasons for forming a government.

The Bill of Rights made it clear that the nation
was not created to be a strict theocracy.

Statements in the Declaration of Independence and Constitution that referred to the Creator and divinely provided rights
also indicated the intention of preserving a place—protected
from state encroachment—for religion, spirituality, informed
public policy, and corporate virtue. The Declaration said people
"are endowed by the Creator with certain unalienable rights"
and appealed to the "Supreme Judge of the world" to examine
the "rectitude of our intentions," as it listed its reasons to declare
America independent from England. To this was added the
crucial Bill of Rights—including separation of church and state.
It was the Federalist answer to anti-Federalist objections to the
Constitution, protecting individual rights from the possibility
of a return to an overwhelming government, even a possibility
for a government without a king. The Bill of Rights secured passage of that new and revolutionary Constitution. In elevating
the individual and his or her rights, conscience was king, but
God was also invoked.[4] Government policy would be negotiated, but freedoms would be protected from a government that
could overwhelm.

Scripture Does Not Inform Governmental Structures

As we think about our government in relationship to Scripture,
we need to address two biblical structures that do not dictate
our government's structure.

First, we consider Israel. Israel was created to be a theocracy. There was only one Israel, and there's no indication in Scripture that earthly governments are to be modeled after Israel. Even as we apply biblical *values* to our country, Scripture does not tell us to apply the *structures* of ancient Israel to the structures of the United States.

Second, the biblical structure of the church does not dictate a Christian's place in public space that is America. In fact, the presence of the church complicates this relationship. The church is not even a nation, as Israel was. It is a commonwealth of heaven existing among and across the nations, interpenetrating a variety of political nations with a community dedicated to honoring and serving God.

The church is sacred space present within and distinct from the public space of a nation. Those who attach themselves to the church *choose* to enter into that sacred space alongside their presence in public space. They do so in part because people who enter sacred space choose to live differently than people in public space.

What is more, the American government chose a route that placed a limit on what religion can do in government. That choice helped to set up the difference between public space and sacred space. Religious values could inform discussion, but religious structures would not be mandated. So reflecting on biblical values does not inform or underwrite our specific governmental structure. Rather, Scripture informs our *interpersonal* and *community* values and asks how they attach to the issues at hand. State versus federal rights, as well as many other issues of the specific logistics of policy, are not directly addressed in Scripture. So when we look through a biblical lens, discussion of structures does not inform the intersection of policy and values.

SCRIPTURE DOES INFORM
HOW WE LIVE TOGETHER

As we look at scriptural teachings on getting along, we will understand why the Bible has had such a profound influence on Western culture. If we really desire to know what Jesus wants for our country, we will look at what Scripture says about mutual regard and accountability to a reality greater than ourselves. Jesus exhorts us to relate to one another out of commandments that call us to love God and our neighbor.

Those who know God in the context of forgiveness have the capacity to forgive others in a way that is distinct from the normal way the world works. In Matthew 5:43–47 and Luke 6:27–38, Jesus calls those who respond to him to love their enemies and live in a way that is distinct from how those in the world often react. This capability changes how the church should respond to political realities. It also pictures a fresh way for how people relate to one another.

Scripture paints a realistic picture of human failure as well as hope for a more perfect world. It points to a way through human limitations, a way supplied by a humble regard of God's grace, by a concern to live with a virtue that honors God and others, and by a desire to serve the community we are in so people of diverse backgrounds can flourish.

Serve Whatever Community You Are In

A wonderful example of this core value of serving whatever community we are in is found in Jeremiah 29:7. This verse is part of a letter the prophet wrote as people from Israel were being exiled to Babylon. These Israelites were headed into life as a minority. They were headed to live in a place full of evil. Still the prophet urged them to pursue their normal lives. The key verse gives a somewhat surprising instruction for how to survive as a minority in an environment that might also prove to be hostile to its values: *"Seek the welfare of the city I have deported you to. Pray to the LORD on its behalf, for when it has prosperity you will prosper."* (HCSB) Similar to the call in Genesis 1 for humanity to reflect God and care well for the creation, so here Jeremiah calls on the faithful to be faithful in seeking and laboring for the benefit of the city where they exist as exiles. The previous verses had them building homes, planting gardens, and creating new marriages and families. They were called upon to multiply in their new home and to contribute to the community there. This verse sets forth that even when one is a stranger in a foreign land, even a hostile land, the best policy is to contribute to the welfare of the place you live.

"Seek the welfare of the city I have deported you to. Pray to the LORD on its behalf, for when it has prosperity you will prosper." —Jeremiah 29:7

Effective versus Ineffective Living

So how do we examine the values that Jesus and Scripture ask us to consider? Scripture portrays success and failure in terms of effective and ineffective living before God and others. It challenges our imagination and heart with a call to moral excellence, or virtue, and with examples of success and failure in its application. It shows a world in pain and projects a world of potential. By precept, priorities, and practice, it calls us to live and relate the present and conflicting elements of life in a fallen, imperfect world in a way that leads to a life lived in conformity to God's character. It examines the interaction between love, justice, peace, wisdom, foolishness, allegiance, idolatry, service, selfishness, accountability, responsibility, productiveness, poverty, wealth, power, impotence, and waste, just to name a few of the values it describes and examines.

Built for Relationship

Scripture says that from the beginning, our world was built for relationships. As a trinity, God himself is a self-related being; and by making us in his image, he designed us not only as stewards of the creation but as beings called to relate well to one another. As God-believers, our faith absolutely must inform how we relate to one another—specifically, when we disagree with one another's politics.

None of this may make sense to a secularist, but this ethic inherently connects us to our fellow humans with a mutual concern and responsibility for one another. Our selfish choices and imbalanced allegiances are disruptive to wholesome relationships. We all fail at relationships, but the goal is to reach for the world as it could be.

Much of Scripture discusses the to and fro of relationship tensions and conflicts. The account of Jesus calls us to sacrifice rather than play for power. His personal sacrifice bore the consequences of our failures so that we could be changed—so that a character of honoring God and loving others could be wrought in each of us. Jesus also said that all the commandments of God are summarized in two simple ideas: loving God completely and loving your neighbor as yourself. This outward versus inward focus and its call to care about others runs counter to many individualistic or tribal trends in our current culture. This otherworldly outward focus might just set the stage for a way forward.

On Government as a Social Contract

Jesus spoke often about how we are to love and care for one another. Our government has somewhat implemented this teaching in that it is a social contract regarding how we come together and live as a union. James Madison, in appealing for the creation of a Bill of Rights to the proposed Constitution, said it this way: "First, that there be prefixed to the constitution a declaration that all power is originally vested in, and consequently derived from the people. That government is instituted, and ought to be exercised for the benefit of the people, which consists in the enjoyment of life and liberty, with the right of acquiring and using property, and generally of pursuing happiness and safety."[5] Our Constitution is about corporate self-government in which all possess core rights simply because we were created with a dignity we received from our Creator. In sum, when we live under this social contract, every citizen has a right to be at the table, to participate in, and be protected by the union the people have formed.

Every citizen has a right to be at the table, to participate in, and be protected by the union the people have formed.

The refusal to create a state religion proclaimed that diversity is a given. This right extended even to those who did not hold to the existence of a Creator. Even though disbelief in God undercut one of the foundations for establishing a sense of virtue and morality, it was affirmed that this union would tolerate such a range of diversity. So how do we have a union with such diversity? How do we hold our social contract together so it remains sustainable? How do we avoid a descent into tribalism, where each special interest looks out only for itself?

The Division of Power

Diversity can lead either to chaos or opportunity. Holding a social contract together in a diverse world is no easy task. In fact, it is a decidedly uneasy one. Sides form and special interest groups fund the efforts to persuade. The temptation to treat anyone with an opposing view as a demagogue is great. Add to that a system where freedom and liberty are the driving traits, and power can be acquired in a way that tilts toward a majority. Then the contract can go anywhere majority passion or choice leads, overriding the freedoms of the minority. The only check in this environment is a recognition and respect for the rights of others as well as my own. In a social contract, trusting people to consider the freedoms of everyone assumes the best of humanity.

Yet this government was formed with the crucial realization that people are not always at their best. In fact, the normal tendency of humans is to think only of themselves and their own self-interest. This very realistic core understanding about people led the framers of our government to divide power so it would never be too concentrated, where concern for the minority was protected. That doctrine was called the *separation of powers*. The executive, legislative, and judiciary branches were set up to operate with divided power. The system became known as checks and balances.

Human Nature to Be Selfish

Our forefathers had fought a revolution to free themselves from a king, who held most of the power. And they knew that humans are prone to be selfish, abuse power, and do what is not best—a truth taught clearly in Scripture. John Adams says it this way in his *A Defense of the Constitutions of Government of the United States of America*:

> But the nature of mankind is one thing, and the reason of mankind another; and the first has the same relation to the last as the whole to the part. The passions and appetites are part of the human nature as well as reason and moral sense. In the institution of government it must be remembered that, although reason ought always to govern individuals, it certainly never did since the Fall, and never will til the Millennium; and human nature must be taken as it is, as it has been, and will be.

In a sermon before the House of Representatives of Massachusetts on October 5, 1780, the New England reverend Samuel Cooper also noted the importance of virtue and the risk of being governed by the people. He told the legislators:

> Virtue is the Spirit of a republic; for where all power is derived from the people, all depends on their good disposition. If they are impious, factious and selfish; if they are abandoned to idleness, dissipation, luxury, and extravagance; if they are lost to the fear of God, and the love of country, all is lost.

Human Capacity to Rise Above

On the other side of the human ledger stood a belief in a common grace, the capacity of people to rise above their selfishness and do what is right. Paul spoke of this common grace in Romans 2:14–16 when he said that Gentiles had a law within themselves even though they did not have the Law of Sinai. This law was written on their hearts and was a reflection of a sensitive conscience and the ability to think beyond ourselves. It is from this place—knowing that we are all created in God's image—that we can begin the pursuit of the common good, not only as a goal of good governing but also as a necessity for a functioning diverse society.

THE CHARACTER OF A SOCIETY

We think all too little about character in our society. Schools teach us knowledge and skill but do not aim at character. In a society where families are often fragmented and religion is marginalized, no one takes on this task. We are materialistic in our approach to education, teaching knowledge as a commodity, but we fail to teach how the person is to use that knowledge. Too many grow up without consideration of the soul and why they do what they do. These are what T. S. Eliot called the "hollow men" of the modern world.

We get what we pay for in this approach to society, because liberty can be destructive if used poorly. The motto at the University of Pennsylvania is right: "Without morality, laws are empty." Pursuing the common good may mean stepping back from our personal sense of the ideal. But the role of genuine conversation alongside confrontation on differences is necessary in a diverse culture. Because we value diversity, we need to guard freedom of speech. For the same reason, we need to protect religious liberty and freedom of conscience.

Pursuing the common good may mean stepping back from our personal sense of the ideal.

In a diverse society, reflecting on character and virtue provides opportunities to evaluate our tensions. That is the hope that undergirds this book: I want it to help all of us evaluate our political positions in light of the actual teachings of Jesus and the Bible, as well as to consider how we have those discussions and debates.

RESPONSIBILITY TO "mend the world" and serve the common good is inscribed into the very character of Christianity as a prophetic religion; it is a consequence of the commitment to love both the one God and neighbors. But in the future, Christians will likely exert that influence less from the centers of power and more from the social margins. Moreover, whether they find themselves close to the centers or far from them, in a religiously and culturally pluralistic world, Christian communities will be only one of many players.

—MIROSLAV VOLF, *A PUBLIC FAITH: HOW FOLLOWERS OF CHRIST SHOULD SERVE THE COMMON GOOD*

2

Starting Points

Loving Your Neighbor

W HEN THINKING about the common good, where do we start? How do we rise above our own self-interest to consider the common good? Thinking about the purpose of life and why we are here may guide us to the common good.

FAITH IN A CREATOR DEFINES PURPOSE OF LIFE

Discussion on the purpose of life becomes very difficult if there is no Creator. Without a Creator, life has no real purpose or design. Everyone else on the planet can become a competitor for the things I want. Atheism or secularism can lead not so much to blasphemy as to purposelessness and tribalism. Negotiating out of self-interest is all I bring to the table if I don't believe in a Creator. Accommodating others is about the best I can do. This mindset offers but a slender thread by which to hold community together.

Faith in a Creator who is responsible for my life and to whom I am responsible adds purpose to the framing and definition of life. As a believer, I am one piece in a larger world puzzle, and I am attached to others whom God has created. I share this globe with others whose existence is made sacred because they are a product of divine design. Life matters and so do lives.

I share this globe with others whose existence is made sacred because they are a product of divine design.

Shakespeare, in *As You Like It*, said we are "merely players" on a global stage,[1] but each one of us is designed to contribute something to the play.

When it comes to this big picture, Scripture gives us three key anchoring points: stewardship, love that pursues justice, and accountability. All three triangulate to help us think about how we should live with and serve our neighbors. Most of the world speaks of the middle trait, love, as if that is all there is, holding to the standard the Beatles used to sing. But without a sense of the other two anchors, love simply floats in midair searching for a place to dwell.

STEWARDSHIP: WHY CREATION MATTERS

In all the debate over Genesis 1 and creation versus evolution, one big thing often goes missing: the point of this grand opening chapter of Scripture. The point ultimately is not about when or how the creation happens but *why*. The text not only says we are creatures in a world of design and purpose, it even tells us what man's mandate is within that creation. The first command from God to people was, *"Be fruitful and multiply! Fill the earth and subdue it! Rule over the fish of the sea and the birds of the air and every creature that moves on the ground"* (Genesis 1:28). So God's mandate, or call, is that we manage the earth, be good stewards of the house God has given us to live in, and multiply and subdue the earth.[2] All of us have this calling. This commission from creation explains in a major way why we are here.

Genesis 1:26–27 tells us something about how God created us: *"Then God said, 'Let us make humankind in our image, after our likeness, so they may rule over the fish of the sea and the birds of the air, over the cattle, and over all the earth, and over all the creatures that move on the earth.' God created humankind in his own image, in the image of God he created them, male and female he created them."*

We are creative creatures because God created us in his image. This creativity leads to art, beauty, literature, athletic skill, creative design, caring, and mutual nurturing. It allows us to ponder, worship, sing, cry, mourn, and rejoice. In short, it is what makes our lives different from animals' or plants'. I often ask: Who has been to the First Methodist Church of Dolphins or a synagogue of butterflies or the First Baptist Church of Robins? Our ability to be self-reflective and creative is unmatched by other creatures. This distinction is a major clue for the purpose of life. We are created as creative, social beings, designed for relationship and community. Built into God's mandate that we subdue the earth is a call to relate to people who are different from us and to work with them to subdue the earth.

We are created for responsibility and with the ability to creatively manage God's gift of the world. God's goal was that humankind manage this creation with skill, peace, creativity, and justice. The disruption came about when Adam and Eve chose to go it alone without God and on their own terms. The first sign that things were amiss was when Cain slew Abel. The power to be creative and free to choose became the choice to be self-destructive and be full only of self-interest. However we see Genesis, its depiction of the purpose, potential, and dangers of the human condition ring true.

LOVE: SEEKING SOLUTIONS BEYOND MYSELF

Love is about more than tolerance; it relates and engages. Love appreciates the complexity of juggling love and self-interest, and it realizes that disagreement can be sincere. Those who call for civility in our social discourse must do more than appeal for its need. Civil discourse only happens when we appreciate and are concerned for our fellow citizens. Patriotism is not seen in the political position I hold, but in how I view my fellow citizens, even in a context of disagreement. One of the reasons our public discourse has broken down is that we have lost this deep sense of love and any sense of mutual respect. What often happens is that we call others to love and respect when we propose our view, yet call the one who disagrees with us an enemy.

Jesus' call to love our enemies is one of his most discussed teachings. It is a perspective that is not only uncommon, but that represents a challenge to all our instincts to be self-focused. In the exhortations surrounding this teaching, Jesus explains this kind of love through acts of service to his enemies.

Love also pursues the biblical virtue of *justice*. Justice is grounded in an appreciation for the sacredness of life and the willingness to treat others as we ourselves want to be treated. Love functions out of a shared human concern and sensitivity toward others.

Pursuit of justice and the common good is most effective in a context of actually loving others. Love argues for principles it considers best for people as a whole, and must seek solutions that extend beyond the self. Ultimately, real love is others-directed. Truth does not always reside in one corner. Because no one is omniscient, blind spots exist. Points of view cover the map. Since love is often mixed with self-interest, sometimes our view is as much about ourselves as about others.

Justice is grounded in an appreciation for the sacredness of life.

Profound love engages with the opposition, but does so respectfully, keeping to the issue and avoiding personal attack. It is possible for us to contend earnestly for a point of view without getting personal. Yet much of our public discussion and media niches undercut genuine discussion. However, loving regard understands that pursuing the common good also means pushing against our tendency to tar our opponent.

Love provides hope of genuine dialogue and listens to what others in the room are saying. Love feeds into justice and a sense of fairness toward my neighbor. Love is willing to grant others the consideration we ask for ourselves. Without love and respect, we will not pursue justice.

ACCOUNTABILITY: A CHECK ON TOTAL LIBERTY

Before the American Revolution, Thomas Paine made this observation about government in his work *The Rights of Man*: "A body of men, holding themselves accountable to nobody, ought not to be trusted by anybody." He understood the dangers of unchecked freedom and unchecked power. Os Guinness titled a recent book *A Free People's Suicide: Sustainable Freedom and the American Future*.[3] His thesis was that Americans love freedom, but freedom without constraints and accountability is suicidal for a society. He went as far as to say, "The greatest enemy of freedom is freedom."[4] Benjamin Franklin in his *Poor Richard's Almanack* said this: "Nothing brings more pain than too much pleasure; nothing more bondage than too much liberty."

Accountability is essential for a sustained society—whether that accountability is based on standards received from God or rooted in a reasoned sense of nobility about how humans should live. Without accountability, freedom becomes license. Knowing the difference between responsible freedom and unrestrained freedom is important to a society's well-being and its pursuit of the common good.

Accountability is a sustaining starting point in the pursuit of the common good. Accountability doesn't ask if something is permissible but if it is beneficial. As Paul said in 1 Corinthians 10:23–24, *"Everything is permitted, but not everything is beneficial. Everything is permitted, but not everything edifies. Do not seek your own good, but the good of the other person."* (Author's translation.)

This kind of accountability reinforces love and leads to good stewardship, and it sets the stage for meaningful dialogue, even healthy disputation.

But What about Conviction?

Being willing to engage with those we disagree with does not mean that positions and convictions don't matter. They *do* matter. But the point of loving engagement is to consider compromise, to be willing to back off.

Being willing to engage with those we disagree with does not mean that positions and convictions don't matter.

Full engagement from all sides means coming to the table and vigorously making your case, but it also means being open to the possibility—no matter how slight you think it is—that the other person may have something valuable to say. Full engagement means listening to opposing views with some level of respect, rather than only trumpeting your approach. As Proverbs 27:17 says, *"As iron sharpens iron, so one person sharpens another."* (NIV)

My email inbox is full of political material both from the right and the left. I'm not sure how I got identified with both wings, but somehow I am perceived as a supporter of both sides. These emails serve to build walls and call on me to dig in and advocate for their position. But my role as a citizen is to thoughtfully assess the proposed positions rather than blindly affirming and supporting them.

Of course, we may come to an impasse on some issues, where bridging the divide is not possible. But on many issues the divide can be bridged or at least ameliorated in ways that allow us to function better side by side. Many differences remain at impasse because we lack actual engagement and there is a dearth of creativity and genuine effort to find a third way. Is our advocacy about our convictions so set in concrete that we cannot seek options that may work for a larger group? More importantly, should we be so immovable? And on topics that are not directly addressed in Scripture, is it right for people of faith to propound their political views as biblical truths?

So when it comes to convictions, all sides should make their case. Our society needs vigorous discussion and the freedom to express opposing views. But all of us need to be in the assessment mode—no one is right about everything. Be willing to listen and hear, not just advocate. Be willing to assess what matters and what can be discussed. Come to the table, and let us reason together.

Practicing *good stewardship*, *engaging love*, and a sense of *mutual accountability* helps set relational parameters for difficult dialogues about differences. These starting points pave a way out of gridlock—not as matters of ideology but as matters of relational citizenship. Without such reference points and commitments, little will change about how we do our political business.

W<small>E HAVE</small> now reached the point where no sooner do Americans send their representatives to Washington than they turn on the Washington that they claim no longer represents them. The core problem can be expressed like this: Such is our human propensity for self-love—or thinking and acting with self at the center—that the virtue it takes for citizens to remain free is quite unnatural. America today is a republic in which the private trumps the public, consumerism tells America, "it's all about me," and citizens constantly tell the government to "get off our backs" when the government is their own justly chosen representative and it supposedly governs only with their free consent. In such a world, self-love will always love itself supremely, love itself at the expense of others and love itself without limits. Thus in Montesquieu's words, the self-renunciation needed for freedom is "always a very painful thing."

—OS GUINNESS, *A FREE PEOPLE'S SUICIDE*

3

Starting Points

Big Government or Small?

THE DEBATE over big versus little government, over states' rights versus federal rights is as old as the move from the failed Articles of Confederation (which originally governed America) to our current Constitution. As that move was being made, the Federalist Papers were produced to make the case for national government.

At this time, government's purpose was relatively simple: to raise up armies for the nation's defense, promote commerce for the general welfare, strive to maintain peace, and negotiate with other nations. As our culture has changed, the pursuit of the general welfare and justice has led to concerns about equal rights, the provision of roads, education, and care for citizens—including social security and health care. Such moves have been and are points of contention in the battle to contain the expanse and expense of government. Big government comes at the ex-pense of personal liberty and requires extensive resources to

make the corporate endeavor workable. The resources required
for the corporate good brings us to this question: Is everything I
earn for my own use and benefit, or do I give part of my wealth
to the government for a larger corporate benefit?

Is everything I earn for my own use and benefit,
or do I give part of my wealth to the government
for a larger corporate benefit?

As with all such tensions, this is not a case of either/or but
a question of the relationship and balance between competing
rights and responsibilities. So let's look to the Bible to see if it
speaks to whether government should do more than merely
protect our personal well-being and regulate commerce.

THE EXAMPLE OF ISRAEL AND
CHURCH COMMUNITIES

A scriptural look at Israel and church communities gives us
insight into whether government should do more than merely
protect our personal well-being and regulate commerce. The
two great commandments of Scripture—to love God and to
love one's neighbor—automatically expand our view beyond
our personal well-being. So what does such a love look like at a
corporate level?

The Old Testament prophet Micah sheds some light: *"[God]
has told you what is good and what it is the LORD requires of you:
to act justly, to love faithfulness, and to walk humbly with your
God"* (Micah 6:8 HCSB). The starting point of mutual account-

ability before God and one another is embedded in God's call to justice. Justice is about honoring the humanity and divine image in each of us. It leads to a concern for fairness, an absence of exploitation, and a commitment not to do anything that yields corporate damage. Justice is individual freedom under the constraint of consideration of my neighbor. It involves a humility that also points beyond self and toward accountability.

Justice in the prophets is about not taking advantage of another, especially financially, and about showing compassion.

Amos 2:6–7 declares: *"I will not relent from punishing Israel for three crimes, even four, because they sell a righteous person for silver and a needy person for a pair of sandals. They trample the heads of the poor on the dust of the ground and block the path of the needy."* (HCSB) When we don't care for others, we stray twice: we move away from God and toward ourselves.

When God railed against Israel through Hosea, the prophet declared, *"There is no truth, no faithful love, and no knowledge of God in the land! Cursing, lying, murder, stealing, and adultery are rampant; one act of bloodshed follows another. For this reason the land mourns and everyone in it languishes"* (Hosea 4:1–3 HCSB). When a society becomes unreliable in its personal relationships and destructive in its interactions, it becomes not only a dangerous place to be but self-destructive as a community.

In contrast to the recipients of Hosea's indictment stands the Law's call to care for people, even those who were not a part of their people. Two texts in Leviticus say it vividly. Leviticus 19:10 says, *"You must not pick your vineyard bare, and you must not gather up the fallen grapes of your vineyard. You must leave them for the poor and the foreigner. I am the LORD your God."* Leviticus 19:33–34: *"When a foreigner resides with you in your land, you must not oppress him. The foreigner who resides with you must be to you like a native citizen among you; so you must love him as yourself, because you were foreigners in the land of Egypt. I am the LORD your God."*

Interestingly, the basis for the Leviticus exhortation was the reminder that the Israelites had been slaves in Egypt. God is telling them not to treat the foreigners among them as they were treated by the Egyptians. All people have a value as human beings that transcends nationality.

Governing is about more than law; it's about how people relate to one another. The question before us is not whether a government is big or small or what government we should have, but whether our government and laws regulate how we treat others, whether those others are citizens or not.

The question before us is not whether a government is big or small or what government we should have, but whether our government and laws regulate how we treat others, whether they are citizens or not.

The clearest biblical text on governing in the New Testament is found in Romans 13:1–7. Here, Paul presents the ideal of what government is to do as he urges believers to be good citizens, subject to governing authorities. He says that those who rule are not concerned with good conduct, but with bad. Those who rule are seen as God's servants in contributing to social order as the bearer of a sword. Citizens are to pay taxes to support the state's work. Rulers are to be shown respect and honor for what they do. And these exhortations were to a people under the rule of an emperor, not the ruler of a nation committed to sacred practice. Paul describes government servants as bearers of a sacred trust because they rule within God's sovereignty (vv. 1–2).

In Acts 2:44 we see a picture of how the church community shared its resources with one another: *"All who believed were together and held everything in common."* This kind of core community goal parallels Deuteronomy 15:4, which says, *"There need be no poor people among you."* (NIV) Matthew 25:35–40 has a similar thrust, when Jesus says that when we show kindness to others, we show kindness to him. Yet another example of community relations is seen in Acts 6, where some complained about a segment of the community that was being ignored on ethnic grounds. In response, that community immediately went about fixing the problem. Such standards were not unique to the church. Jewish communities, as well as those in the Greek world, sensed that they should care for those in their midst.[1]

Because Israel and the church were models for how people should live together in community, the extension of their community goals into more general contexts is appropriate.

As we discuss community care we must balance that discussion with community responsibility. Here's what the Bible says on that side of the discussion: 2 Thessalonians 3:10–13 speaks against people who are idle and says, *"The one who is unwilling to work shall not eat."* The "idlers" are to seek to make a living. They are to show responsibility.

So a community is to be generous enough to see that core needs are met, but those who receive help should seek ways to support themselves and even help others. The ability of a person to help does not negate the responsibility of the receiver to work. And a lack of responsibility does not remove the obligation to help. In fact, the one able to help is to err on the side of generosity—even going so far as to help the one in need to become more self-sustaining. The person who can help the one in need should do so, just as the one in need should move to get out of need. What is interesting about such exhortations is that they do not cross paths. The one who is asked to be generous is not asked to throw responsibility in the face of the one in need, and the one who needs to show responsibility is not told to tell others to be generous. Each is responsible before God to give what he or she can.

As Jesus said, society will always contain people who are "poor" or in need of aid (Matthew 26:11). Ideally, the needs of these people would be met without government aid or entitlement to other resources the society has; but the emphasis of many biblical texts is on being sure that governments or communities provide for people's core needs. Community calls us to care for others beyond ourselves and consider more than what our own rights permit. In aiming toward such goals, there is more than the role of government to consider.

SEPARATION OF CHURCH AND STATE

American government is neither a theocracy nor is it a state-church alliance. The government our framers crafted functioned with religious beliefs flanking and serving alongside culture and government. The benefit of this structure is that nationalism and religion could be more easily separated. In this structure, a person comes to religious faith—not as a matter of birth or compulsion—but by a conscious choice. A person chooses what sacred space to occupy, including whether to occupy it at all. Even God allows people to choose their own way, even if it harms them. This is Jesus' picture of the prodigal son in Luke 15:11–32. This son initially is allowed to go his own way, even to his own detriment.

The beauty of the separation of church and state is that the church can function on its own. It can have its own identity and form its own internal subculture where each expression of faith can follow its own set of social and moral commitments. It can reflect community in ways distinct from the larger, more variegated culture. It can also be energized and respond to needs in the culture with less red tape and bureaucracy than government.

Hurricane Katrina provided a vivid illustration of the different ways the government and churches can help. The devastation from that storm stretched everyone responsible for offering relief, especially relief for those who were displaced. As is common in times of disaster, the government came in to offer what aid it could, but coordinating all of its entities across all levels proved complicated, especially since many of the city's homeless had to be moved to other cities in order to be cared for. Numerous religious organizations mobilized to help with food and shelter, not to mention helping people rebuild their homes and lives. This example shows what can happen when the church and other religious organizations come alongside the government with their compassionate muscle. It reflects common labor for the common good.

Disasters force us to drop our differences and reach out to help in whatever way we can. Tragedies drive us to become less selfish and more others-centered. These events demonstrate what people are capable of in their best moments—when we instinctively sense the core human need, we are driven to work as hard for others as we can.

The lesson here is that government cannot do everything required, but the reverse is also true—religious and other relief organizations dedicated to compassion cannot do everything either.

WHAT GOVERNMENT SHOULD *DO* VERSUS WHAT IT SHOULD *BE*

The lesson of the Katrina example is that when we think about and debate what government should *do* versus what government should *be* as it serves its people, we fail to focus on what values our laws should reflect. When we focus on the *doing*, we risk breaking ourselves up into special interest groups that drive for their piece of the pie, without considering the needs of others.

Government cannot do everything required, but the reverse is also true—religious and other relief organizations cannot do everything either.

When we simply ask what government should or should not *do*, we lose the focus on what government should or should not *be*. James Skillen, in his book *The Good of Politics*, says it this way:

> Individual Americans and both profit-making and non-profit organizations all want the government to do (or not do) certain things to benefit them. The major political parties, which help support candidates for elections, are not built on philosophies of what the republic should be but on a collection of things their supporters want government to do. . . . As a consequence, legislators are pushed to become brokers of multiple interests rather than public servants held accountable by a national electorate for the republic's long-term well-being.[2]

Big Government or Small:
A Look at the Debate

Let's try to ask the right questions as we do some critical assessment about the size of government. In an article for the *National Review*, Michael Tanner makes the case against big government.[3] He makes five points and backs them up with data:

- Big Government is unaffordable.
- Big Government is incompatible with economic growth.
- Big Government does not work.
- Big Government breeds corruption.
- Big Government limits freedom.

For example, under point 3, Tanner argues, "Government intervention crowds out the private actions of civil society, which are far more effective in addressing people's needs. Big government doesn't only make it harder to care for ourselves and our families; it also makes it harder to care for our fellow man."

Here is his closing point: "This is why the fight over the size of government really matters. Big government leaves us poorer and less prosperous. And it fails to alleviate our social ills. But most significantly, big government denies the unique value and self-worth of every individual. And that is why, on both the left and right, those who would try to harness big government to their own ends will ultimately fail."

This position argues that big government doesn't work, but it is hard-pressed to answer the question of how social needs will be met if government does not address them. Might the absence of governmental involvement result in people being worse off?

On the other side of the political ledger are those who contend for big government. A website of Dr. Douglas Amy, professor of Politics at Mount Holyoke College, makes such a case.[4] He gives responses to the kind of criticisms Tanner raises. Here is a sample of his list and responses:

- *Criticism:* Government is inept and most government policies fail.

  Response: A look at the record shows that most government programs work well and have helped considerably to mitigate society's problems and improve our lives.

- *Criticism:* Government only interferes with the efficient operation of a market economy. Capitalism would be better off without government.

  Response: Free-market capitalism could not exist without an active government that provides the extensive legal infrastructure that creates and regulates markets and that enables corporations to do business.

- *Criticism:* The more government programs we have, the less freedom we have.

  Response: Most government programs—such as fire protection, building roads, food stamps, public education, funding scientific research, and Social Security—do virtually nothing to restrict our individual freedoms.

- *Criticism:* Government regulations often cost more than the benefits they produce.[5]

  Response: The benefits to society from regulations almost always outweigh their economic costs.

THE RIGHT QUESTIONS

It is interesting to note that the affordability issue is not directly addressed in any of Amy's responses. All he offers is a claim that the benefits outweigh the costs, which does not directly discuss affordability. On the other hand, the economic impact is central for Tanner.

So it seems in this debate that the real issue is what we are willing to pay or can afford to pay for the common good. A key issue is whether we are willing to extend our resources and make individual sacrifices so that all of us are better cared for.

Our discussion need not have an "all or nothing" approach. But it does require getting into details about feasibility versus value. It means that real political dialogue has to dig down into the data and move beyond the slogans and summaries that often direct political debate and the ads that seek to persuade. Part of the discussion also has to raise the question: If government does not do it, should we? Is our society willing to tackle such a need independent of government? Can and should the needs of others go unaddressed?

If we are asking questions about the efficiency and affordability of government meeting core needs, the answer might be to allow private organizations to at least provide some of the aid.

But if we are asking questions about the values that make our society better for the common good, there are other legitimate questions that also need attention: (1) What values determine what our government and society should strive to be? (2) How much should I be willing to sacrifice for the betterment of the whole? (3) If government does not take up this human concern, then where and how will it be addressed and does that alternative have a real chance of doing it better and in a more efficient way?

Biblical values do not address what the structure of government ought to be, but they do consistently raise value questions about how I care for and love my neighbor. The tension in this topic is how do we best get there. It tells us that politics may not be as much about opposing views as it is about balancing tensions that need alignment.

THE BIBLE treats economics as a moral issue. It is full of stories and commands that have a lot to do with economics. Though Jesus had little to say about economic systems, He had a lot to say about economic life—about wealth, possessions, and personal morality—but a lot less about economic systems. . . . Capitalism provides the resources that are necessary for either private charity, or public assistance through taxes to help support the poor. Both charity and government assistance assume productive wealth creation. Otherwise where do the resources come from to help the poor? But, more importantly, capitalism provides opportunities for the poor to help themselves out of poverty and uphold their dignity at the same time, since they are participants in the system and not simply recipients of charity.

—AUSTIN HILL AND SCOTT RAE,
THE VIRTUES OF CAPITALISM

4

Economics and Poverty

Personal Wealth or Shared Resources?

THE PERSONAL freedom to accumulate wealth is an important concern as we look at government. Biblical values address both our freedom to accumulate wealth and our obligation to help others. How we balance these values is a major concern of Scripture.

So as we consider the individual use of resources, we will consider (1) the texts that affirm wealth, (2) what Scripture says about the dangers inherent in its accumulation, and (3) how these principles can be applied to money on a corporate or community level.

BIBLICAL AFFIRMATION OF WEALTH

Scripture does not condemn wealth per se. In fact, wealth is often affirmed and seen as a blessing from God. What the Bible condemns is how one abuses it.

Wealth properly used is seen as a blessing. Ecclesiastes 5:19 says, "*When God gives someone wealth and possessions, and the ability to enjoy them, to accept their lot and be happy in their toil—this is a gift of God.*"

Proper use of wealth includes the need to provide for one's family—food, shelter, clothing, health care, and other core needs of life—which in the modern world might include education to further equip oneself to contribute to society. This is part and parcel of stewarding the earth: using our resources positively to care for those around us and "*especially for [our] own household*" (1 Timothy 5:8). The goal is that we not be a drain on society but do our part in serving our community (2 Thessalonians 3:8).

Proverbs associates riches with wisdom. Proverbs 3:16 places riches in wisdom's hand: "*Long life is in her right hand; in her left hand are riches and honor.*" This text is not a promise of prosperity but is about the precious value of wisdom. The text reinforces the value of the right virtues. Proverbs 8:18 says that wisdom has "*enduring wealth and prosperity.*" (NIV) Proverbs 8:19 goes on to declare that what is gained by the wealth of wisdom is greater than pure gold or choice silver. Wisdom is like food that "*feeds many*" (Proverbs 10:21).

Wealth and wisdom combined serve society and contribute to its well-being—often through creatively providing services that help others function more efficiently in their lives. In 2 Chronicles 1:11, God commends Solomon because he asked for wisdom to govern the people of Israel instead of riches. And because Solomon chose wisdom over wealth God says in verse 12, "*Furthermore I am giving you wealth, possessions and honor surpassing that of any king before or after you.*" God's wisdom is the most valuable thing we can possess. Properly applied, his wisdom can lead to material wealth.

The benefits of wealth are also affirmed in the picture of Proverbs 10:15, where wealth is said to be like a fortified city, while poverty brings ruin. In Proverbs, wealth is seen as a product of industrious labor. Proverbs 10:4 says, *"The one who is lazy becomes poor, but the one who works diligently becomes wealthy."* Proverbs 14:23 says that *"in all hard work there is profit, but merely talking about it only brings poverty."* Proverbs 24:30–34 addresses laziness versus industrious work and says, *"A little sleep, a little slumber, a little folding of the hands to relax, and your poverty will come like a bandit, and your need like an armed robber."*

It is texts like these that led many to define the Protestant work ethic as a hard day's work for a solid wage. That work ethic is tied to the dignity of labor found in what God called people to do as stewards, so that the hard worker is compensated in texts like Deuteronomy 25:4 and Luke 10:7. 1 Timothy 5:18 argues: *"For Scripture says, 'Do not muzzle an ox while it is treading out the grain,' and 'The worker deserves his wages.'"* (NIV)

As we see from these biblical texts, the pursuit of riches is not a bad thing. Rather, resources are a blessing when they are used well and when they are used to benefit our families and others in our society.

Resources are a blessing when they are used
well and when they are used to benefit our families
and others in our society.

WHAT SCRIPTURE SAYS ABOUT POTENTIAL DANGERS IN WEALTH ACCUMULATION

There are few themes that run as deep in Scripture as this one, especially among the prophets. Jesus' teaching also dealt with this potential danger. In general, Scripture teaches that wealth is not inherently destructive, but it is quite destructive when it is abused.

The Proverbs

As we've seen, Proverbs has much teaching on the blessings of wealth, but it also warns about its risks. First, riches can all too easily produce a false sense of confidence and security. Proverbs 11:28 says, *"The one who trusts in his riches will fall, but the righteous will flourish like a green leaf."* Another danger of wealth is that it can produce a dangerous kind of self-indulgence. Proverbs 21:17 notes, *"The one who loves pleasure will be a poor person; whoever loves wine and anointing oil will not be rich."*

Further, wealth is sometimes gained by taking advantage of others. Proverbs 22:16 observes, *"The one who oppresses the poor to increase his own gain and the one who gives to the rich—both end up only in poverty."* Here, oppression is described as the *source* of wealth, not wealth as the *cause* of oppression. Both oppressing the poor and cowering to the rich lead to poverty.

The Prophets and Psalms

The prophets also warn against gaining wealth at the expense of others. Jeremiah 5:27 observes, *"Like a cage filled with the birds that have been caught, their houses are filled with the gains of their fraud and deceit. That is how they have gotten so rich and powerful."* Micah 6:12 complains, *"The city's rich men think nothing of resorting to violence; her inhabitants lie, their tongues speak deceptive words."* So Psalm 62:10 warns, *"Do not trust in what you can gain by oppression! Do not put false confidence in what you can gain by robbery! If wealth increases, do not become attached to it!"*

Jesus

Jesus also discussed the topic. In Luke 12:15–21, Jesus tells a parable about a rich farmer who, when his crops increased even more, did not consider and also deliberately avoided giving to others—even building bigger barns to contain all his crop. But because he kept all for himself, God took away his life with the reminder that someone else would get what he'd selfishly hoarded. This man's riches led to a sense of self-sufficiency that drove him away from God.

The fate of another rich man in a parable about a poor beggar named Lazarus takes the same path (Luke 16:19–31). When they both died, Jesus tells us that Lazarus was carried to his reward by angels, while the rich man found himself in hell. This rich man knew who Lazarus was but did not do anything to help him—even though it would have taken little effort or sacrifice. A lack of compassion for the poor is the point of this parable in a chapter that is said to be about money (Luke 16:14 with 19–31).

In yet another text, there is a real-life conversation between Jesus and a rich young ruler (Luke 18:18–30). Here the wealthy man is faced with the choice of selling all and giving the money to the poor or losing eternal life. Jesus was testing how much the man was concerned about others. This man's riches kept him from lasting wealth as he merely walked away.

The Apostle Paul

The apostle Paul plays the same notes of concern about wealth. He associates greed with idolatry (Ephesians 5:5). Here are two pieces of advice about wealth from 1 Timothy 6. Verses 7–10 speak to the ungodly pursuit of wealth:

> We have brought nothing into this world and so we cannot take a single thing out either. But if we have food and shelter, we will be satisfied with that. Those who long to be rich, however, stumble into temptation and a trap and many senseless and harmful desires that plunge people into ruin and destruction. For the love of money is the root of all evils. Some people in reaching for it have strayed from the faith and stabbed themselves with many pains.

Later in the same chapter the advice to those with wealth in verses 17–19 is:

> Command those who are rich in this world's goods not to be haughty or to set their hope on riches, which are uncertain, but on God who richly provides us with all things for our enjoyment. Tell them to do good, to be rich in good deeds, to be generous givers, sharing with others. In this way they will save up a treasure for themselves as a firm foundation for the future and so lay hold of what is truly life.

The values tied to wealth are complex. Wealth is good when it is used to benefit the family and others. And as long as they don't lead to excessive self-focus, monetary resources can help humans flourish and find ways to steward God's creation. The danger is that wealth accumulation often takes advantage of others or leads to a self-interest that sees people as objects that either advance or hinder a wealthy person's selfish pursuits. In such cases, wealth becomes not only self-destructive but impacts society negatively as well. Negotiating these competing options and this tension is part of what society faces when dealing with economics.

FROM INDIVIDUAL TO CORPORATE ECONOMICS

There is little in Scripture that directly addresses corporate economics. This is because most ancient monetary life was built around agriculture, fishing, or skilled labor. Capital development was minimal, as technological innovation was sporadic at best. Service industries were mostly subsumed under forms of slavery and did not contribute to a developing economy. Growing an economy where the pie gets bigger for more was nearly impossible in this structure. A person's social status often froze his or her place in the community, and widespread illiteracy contributed to these limitations.

Shareholding corporations did not exist in ancient Israel, and most business activity was conducted between individuals. In the ancient world, opportunities for the powerful to take advantage of the less powerful abounded and frequently were the case. The principles we see in biblical discussions of interpersonal values serve as a good reference point for our discussion of economics as we look at larger institutions engaged in impersonal exchange in the modern world.

Technological advances didn't emerge until the medieval period, and they intensified with the Industrial Revolution. These advances and their impact continue today. Reflection on wealth and poverty has a rich legacy, extending back to before the Reformation.[1]

Things have changed in important ways since the writing of Scripture.[2] Rapid rates of economic growth and social mobility offer new opportunities for people to start enterprises and engage in trade.[3] And this can be a good thing. Scripture tells us that it is not money that is evil but how we handle it.

Scripture tells us that it is not money
that is evil but how we handle it.

The discussion on larger business is still about how we relate to one another as people. One of the hidden dangers in large business is that individuals are often depersonalized in the pursuit of profit. Another is that those who are most responsible for injustice can hide behind a layer of managers or the size of the operation, not to mention how sheer logistics can complicate effective, humane service. On the other hand, an effective economic system or business can provide society with great benefits.

Once again we are called not to embrace a macro principle that says business is good or business is bad, but to consider the kind of society that businesses build. Character matters and so does motive. Seeking profit and managing resources well are responsibilities of all who are in charge of a business, just as they are for all who govern a nation. How much is enough and how we share what we have obtained are legitimate questions. Issues that fall into these discussions include level of taxes and social benefits, governmental spending on the military, and resources given to environmental care. Discussions are complex because they involve answers at a large national macro level as well as in more localized forms with cities or families.[4] Answers are best negotiated as economics, and needs are balanced through a vigorous discussion of how we can best help one another. Scriptural values about the poor, human flourishing, and justice for all humanity should guide us in our corporate economics.

On the Poor

Political discussions about welfare and government aid of all kinds can be well informed by Scripture, even though the language is different. The themes of justice and love undeniably tell us to care about the poor.

Caring for the Poor

Just judgment is discussed in Leviticus 19:15 and tells the people, *"You must neither show partiality to the poor nor honor the rich. You must judge your fellow citizen fairly."* Justice renders what is due to each person—regardless of their financial level. But we are also exhorted to care for the poor with sensitivity and generosity. The classic illustration of God's care for the poor in ancient Israel was in his command that the corners of fields were to be left for the poor and the foreigner (Leviticus 23:22). Deuteronomy 15:4 said to Israel that *"there should not be any poor among you, for the LORD will surely bless you in the land that he is giving you as an inheritance."* The assumption here is that the proper management of resources provides everyone with enough income to avoid poverty. Other scriptures lay out important principles for caring for the poor:

- The Israelites were exhorted that they *"must not harden your heart or be insensitive to"* the impoverished condition of the poor (Deuteronomy 15:7).
- The God of the Bible is a God who *"raises the poor from the ash heap"* (1 Samuel 2:8).
- *"The one who oppresses the poor insults his Creator, but whoever shows favor to the needy honors him"* (Proverbs 14:31).
- In Amos 4:1, God strongly condemns those who oppress the poor and crush the needy—a refrain that runs through many of the prophets.
- Amos 2:6–8 also condemns those who live luxuriously off the backs of the poor.

It would not be inaccurate to say that a scriptural litmus test for our concern for our neighbor is measured in how we view and treat the poor. That makes poverty a concern for any who are concerned about the human condition.

A scriptural litmus test for our concern for our neighbor is measured in how we view and treat the poor.

The above scriptures are a mere sample of texts from the Old Testament about how to treat the poor. This list could be expanded many times. These readings explain the rich tradition in Judaism and among Jews that the poor should be cared for. It is one of the features in the Judeo-Christian tradition that has made the West a generous and giving culture when it is functioning with sensitivity.

Levels of Assistance

In sensitively dealing with the poor, we need to exercise wisdom regarding the level of help needed to truly help them. In a fascinating book, Steve Corbett and Brian Fikkert discuss engaging poverty in ways that provide real opportunity for the poor to move beyond their need. The book is called *When Helping Hurts: How to Alleviate Poverty without Hurting the Poor.*[5] In it they observe three levels of help for the poor.

The first is called *relief*. This is simply responding to disaster or giving aid that meets the short-term, immediate need. It is what they call an effort "to stop the bleeding." It is the Good Samaritan binding up the wounded man on the road or people sending relief like food and clothing after a natural disaster. The second level is *rehabilitation*, which seeks to restore people to a functional level. It teaches the person being aided how to help with his or her own recovery. The final and more encompassing level is *development*. Here the goal is empowering people to care for themselves. This means enabling individuals to carry out the creation mandate of Genesis 1:26–28 to subdue the earth and be a responsible, disciplined, and caring steward of its resources. It is here that education and affordable care fit, for unless people are equipped to contribute to the world and are healthy enough to do so, their ability to help in the operation and management of our world becomes more difficult.

As Corbett and Fikkert develop these levels of involvement, they go on to say, "One of the biggest mistakes that North American churches make—by far—is in applying relief in situations in which rehabilitation or development is the appropriate intervention."[6] It does not take much to see that the two levels of assistance most needed for long-term help cannot be the responsibility of any single social entity. As a social problem and a social concern, poverty is something all our societal structures need to tackle if we are to have any chance at lessening the problem.

What Jesus Says about Caring for the Poor

In the discussion of the poor, a statement from Jesus is sometimes injected as a way of arguing that the problem is not our concern. When a woman anointed him for burial with precious perfume, the disciples were indignant that she would have "wasted" such expensive perfume instead of selling it and giving the money to the poor. Jesus' response was "For you will always have the poor with you" (Mark 14:7). This statement has been contorted to mean that the poor will always be around, and that's just the way this world is. No big deal. But if we look at the rest of that verse we see that Jesus said, "You will always have the poor with you, and you can do good for them whenever you want. But you will not always have me!" Jesus' remark was not a dismissal of care for the poor; it was a reminder that care for the poor is an ongoing responsibility. In fact, the remark is an allusion to Deuteronomy 15:11: "There will never cease to be poor in the land. Therefore I command you, 'You shall open your hand to your brother, to the needy and to the poor, in your land.'" (ESV)

There can be little doubt that the value of sensitively caring for the poor runs throughout the humanitarian concern Scripture calls on us to have for our neighbor. Jesus himself lived out this ethic, saying he came to reach out to the poor in preaching good news to them (Luke 4:18), and he showed this mission by ministering to those on the fringe of society, as many accounts of his ministry indicate.

- Matthew 19:21 speaks to being generous with our resources as evidence of maturity.
- In Matthew 25:36–44 Jesus equates service to the poor with service to him.
- Luke 14:13 urges us to care for those whom society mostly ignores.

The Responsibilities of the Poor

But justice in regards to the poor cuts two ways: Those who have riches are called to be generous and compassionate in being a good neighbor. But those who are poor should not steal or be envious of what others have legitimately gained. And they are responsible to do what they can to change their situation. The poor are not merely passive recipients. They are to step up and take advantage of the opportunities that rehabilitation and development provide. Scripture has a lot to say about this:

- Those who are lazy are not to be rewarded (2 Thessalonians 3:10).
- The Proverbs frequently challenge the sluggard (Proverbs 6:8; 10:26; 20:4; 22:13; 24:30; 26:14).
- Proverbs 20:4 shows the point *"The sluggard will not plow during the planting season, so at the harvest time he looks for the crop but has nothing."*

A caring society will find ways to provide *and* encourage meaningful labor so all can contribute. Being unemployed eats at the dignity of a person. We are created to labor; and being made in the image of God, we are called to manage what we have. When opportunities for improvement do not readily exist, the fault sometimes lies with society and its structures.

When such opportunities do exist and a person does not take advantage of them, then the fault lies with the person.

We are created to labor; and being made in the image of God, we are called to manage what we have.

This complexity exists because the causes of unemployment are varied. Some people are between jobs, by choice. Others are temporarily unemployed because they have moved or are gaining training to enter a new field. But some lack incentive to find work and choose to take what the government gives them. This kind of unemployment limits how a person contributes to a society. However, when government or private organizations affirm their support by helping people transition from *relief* to *development*, those people are better equipped to contribute to society. This approach encourages the long-term growth of the labor pool and personal development that can serve others.

Complex Issues and Difficult Questions

The topic of the poor is a complex one and raises many difficult questions. For instance, what level of support is society responsible for, and what can society afford to provide? When is poverty no longer poverty? When does development get to the point where people are equipped to be on their own? When a person grows up with little emphasis on the value of education or labor or on personal development, is earlier societal help needed to prevent a longer-term problem? How do our societal and structural problems or obstacles make it hard for many to develop the skills needed to participate in our communities? Whose fault is that? Whose responsibility is it to fix it?

As we can see, there is a real need for balance here, and determining that balance requires reflection and discussion. Governments should be involved in helping the poor do better and make their way.

- In Proverbs 22:22, the city elders at the gate are told not to take advantage of the poor or the afflicted.
- When private judges failed, it was the responsibility of the king to step in (Psalm 72).
- On the other hand, 1 Samuel 8:10–18 warned about kings who would take so much from the people that they would cry out to God for help.

So determining what levels of tax and public support are exorbitant or when government overreaches is appropriate. Balancing personal needs with legitimate corporate concerns lies at the heart of meaningful political dialogue. And those discussions can be undertaken without demonizing the competing options.

So . . . What Would Jesus Say about Accumulating versus Sharing Wealth?

Without being presumptuous, we can put together what Scripture says about this topic and get a pretty clear picture of where Jesus and Scripture stand on this issue. In several passages we've looked at, we see that Jesus emphatically calls society to care for the poor. A multitude of other passages call the poor to take responsibility for their participation in society. In fact, Jesus and the prophets form a kind of echo chamber on this theme, singing the notes repeatedly. As we apply what Scripture says to our society, we come to some essential core values, including:

- giving dignity to labor
- calling for and nurturing responsible contribution to our society
- affirming and adequately rewarding those who work
- emphasizing that most jobs serve our neighbors
- pointing to how we should rejoice in and steward our creation well
- keeping an eye out for injustice and seeking to remove it
- all the while, showing an active, compassionate concern for the poor

As on all difficult issues, we are in serious need of meaningful, balanced discussions about how society should help and how those in need should contribute to that help. We need to be especially sensitive to how opportunity to contribute can be blocked by how our society functions. If we'll try to take stands that reflect the heart of Jesus, we'll avoid cherry-picking arguments that bolster "our side," and consider what conforms to biblical principles. Justice, mercy, compassion, and responsibility can coexist.

THOSE AMERICANS who die or go broke because they happen to get sick represent a fundamental moral decision our country has made. Despite all the rights and privileges and entitlements that Americans enjoy today, we never have decided to provide medical care for everybody who needs it. The far-reaching health care reform that Congress passed in 2010 is designed to increase coverage substantially—but it will still leave about 23 million Americans uninsured. Even when "Obamacare" takes full effect, the American health care system will still lead to large numbers of unavoidable deaths and bankruptcies among our fellow citizens. As we saw in the national debate over that bill, efforts to increase coverage tend to be derailed by arguments about "big government" or "free enterprise" or "socialism"—and the essential moral question gets lost in the shouting.

All other developed countries on earth have made a different moral decision. All the other countries like us—that is, wealthy, technologically advanced, industrialized democracies—guarantee medical care to anyone who gets sick. Countries that are just as committed as we are to equal opportunity, individual liberty, and the free market have concluded that everybody has a right to health care—and they provide it. One result is that most rich countries have better national health care statistics—longer life expectancy, lower infant mortality, better recovery rates from major diseases—than the United States does. Yet all other countries spend far less on health care than the United States does.

—T. R. REID, *THE HEALING OF AMERICA: A GLOBAL QUEST FOR BETTER, CHEAPER, AND FAIRER HEALTH CARE*

5

Health Care

Comprehensive Coverage or Choice?

It would be fair to say that everything we have said about the size of government, affordability, and moral choice comes together in a perfect storm that is called health care. I am reminded of the scene in *The Wizard of Oz* where Dorothy and her three companions face the challenge with a cry of "Lions and tigers and bears, oh my!" Here, the cry is "Doctors and lawyers and insurance, oh my!" The combination of past structures and incredibly powerful, competing special interests have allowed the essential moral question to get lost. That question revolves around the value of human life—which includes quality of life. As Jack Cochran, MD, and Charles Kenney say it in *The Doctor Crisis: How Physicians Can, and Must, Lead the Way to Better Health Care*, "The American Dream is under siege, and health care is a leading barbarian at the gate." [1]

THINKING THROUGH THE MORAL CHOICE

You don't need to read the Bible for long to know that human life matters to God. Life is regarded as precious in all religious traditions. In the Judeo-Christian worldview, it is because people are made in the image of God, giving every life a level of sacred stature:

- Genesis 1:27 says, *"God created humankind in his own image, in the image of God he created them, male and female he created them."*
- Psalm 8:4–9 praises God for the honor he gives to humans and human life: *"Of what importance is the human race, that you should notice them? Of what importance is mankind, that you should pay attention to them, and make them a little less than the heavenly beings? You grant mankind honor and majesty; you appoint them to rule over your creation; you have placed everything under their authority, including all the sheep and cattle, as well as the wild animals, the birds in the sky, the fish in the sea and everything that moves through the currents of the seas. O LORD, our Lord, how magnificent is your reputation throughout the earth!"*
- Psalm 139:13 speaks of God making us, which points to how precious human life is: *"Certainly you made my mind and heart; you wove me together in my mother's womb."* The psalm as a whole is about God taking notice of human life.
- Psalm 78:72 praises David for his care of his people as a king.
- Jeremiah 23:2 condemns leaders for their lack of care for the people, which has allowed them to be dispersed.
- In Luke 10:36–37 we also see this value of life in the par-

abolic picture of the Good Samaritan who bound the wounds of the man who fell among robbers. After telling this parable to a querying lawyer who asked who their neighbor was, Jesus asked him, *"'Which of these three do you think became a neighbor to the man who fell into the hands of the robbers?' The expert in religious law said, 'The one who showed mercy to him.' So Jesus said to him, 'Go and do the same.'"* This parable is a model of the compassion that Jesus urges us to possess.

- Matthew 25:36 commends people for caring for others, including taking care of them when they are sick.
- James 1:27 says that one aspect of pure and undefiled religion is to care for orphans and widows.

For our discussion here, let's assume that life is worth protecting and that the sick are worth helping. The very presence of organizations like the Red Cross or extended relief efforts in the midst of disasters operate on such assumptions about human life. So the matter at hand is how to balance the various factors and entities at work in executing that care and how to move the corporate will to a more compassionate, care-available approach.

For our discussion here, let's assume that life is worth protecting and that the sick are worth helping.

Protecting life and our well-being in this life is supposed to matter. Where there is the threat of fire, we provide a fire department to save lives and protect property. Firemen even risk their lives to save those in danger. Where there is the threat of crime, we provide police to protect life, limb, liberty, and property. Policemen also risk their lives to keep the peace. When a nation is at risk, we provide a military presence to ensure that our citizenry is protected from the threat of invasion, loss of freedom, and loss of life and livelihood. We call this self-defense and protecting our strategic interests. The military services suffer loss of life every year in the pursuit of such protection.

Yet when it comes to medical care and the protection of life through good health policy, insurance companies and those who produce prescription medicines usually care more about their bottom line than the well-being of those they serve. Moral considerations are most often not part of their directing strategy, as profit also becomes a driving concern.

STATISTICS ABOUT HEALTH CARE

Before we look at the different sides of this issue, let's look at some of the research. In the book quoted at the opening of this chapter, the author shares the results of his global study of different health care systems across the world.[2] The statistics are shocking. In 2005 (and things have gotten worse since then), health expenditure as a percentage of GNP was 16.5 percent in the United States. France was next at 11 percent.[3] We lead the world in spending for health care. But, Reid argues, we do not get the appropriate bang for our buck. We are ranked nineteenth in curing people with diseases that are curable with decent care. Our infant mortality rate is the highest among twenty-three wealthy countries and is even behind Cuba, according to the *CIA World Fact Book* (2009).[4]

In 2012, we spent $2.8 trillion on health care. That alone

makes our health care expenditures the fifth largest economy in the world! We spend 40 percent more per person than the next highest country, Norway.[5] Eighteen cents of every US dollar goes to health care.

Our ranking in regards to health care has been consistent since 2005. A recent study released in June 2014 shows that in 2011 the United States had the highest per capita expense in health care ($8,508) of eleven developed countries (Australia, Canada, France, Germany, Netherlands, New Zealand, Norway, Sweden, Switzerland, and the UK). The next highest expenditure-per-capita nation was Norway, at $5,669. In spite of our top-ranking health care costs, we rank last in the quality of care, access, efficiency, equity, and, most important, healthy lives.[6] These statistics were compiled before the recent initiation in 2014 of what has been called Obamacare. In fact, statistics like this are part of the reason it was implemented. It is an attempt to alter this situation. It is too early to tell if this legislation will be successful, but the principles of what could be done are revealed in some of the numbers we cite. Something needed to change. The argument involves more than a debate about big government.

What is evident from these statistics and from our own personal experience is that health care has become cost prohibitive for many and is a big drain on our national economy. Anyone who runs a business or a school knows that underwriting care for employees is one of the most challenging parts of planning and executing a budget. In preparing this chapter, I purchased the recognized books on the economics of this topic. They began with stories about people who could not get access to care because of its cost. Or if they did have access, the cost placed them on the edge of solvency. Emanuel lists four consequences for our level of spending on health care: "(1) more uninsured Americans, (2) cuts to education and other state programs, (3), stagnant wages, and (4) growing federal deficit and debt."[7]

Our country has a tiger by the tail when it comes to health care. We possess a moral sense that people should be able to get care, but we don't know how we can possibly afford it. If any area demands a meaningful, common-good discussion where we balance need and affordability—both important moral imperatives—then it is health care. Most everyone agrees that what we have now does not work economically, as has been shown by the constant rise in health care expense. Balancing health care availability with cost and effective care is a challenge in today's world.

WHAT A TANGLED MESS WE WEAVE

Anyone who gets medical care has to deal with two entities: doctors and insurers. Many people think that the money doctors earn is exorbitant and that drugs are too expensive. Granted, many drug companies price their medications much higher than the cost to produce; however, the fact is that doctors and drug prices are not where the high costs really reside. It takes extensive research, time, and energy to develop the drugs we take, and the cost of paying for technology and health specialists is very high.

Insurers, as we shall see, are largely responsible for the cost of health care in our country. In many ways, they are also the gatekeepers. In the end, they decide who gets care and who does not. The role of insurers in the United States is almost unique among developed countries.

A personal example involves my wife. She had a circulatory

condition that left her in constant pain. Her doctor recommended a hysterectomy, even though she was relatively young. The insurer, looking only at her age, initially refused to pay for the surgery, even though the doctor recommended it. Only after a long haggling process was the surgery approved. All of this time and paperwork is expensive, not to mention the emotional stress of having a doctor tell you a procedure is advised only to have the insurer say they are not paying—putting insurers in the position of health care managers. So doctors treat patients with an eye over their shoulder.

There is another issue in play with insurance: potential malpractice litigation. The pressure this puts on doctors requires them to carry significant malpractice insurance—and in some cases, order tests whose major role is protection from legal exposure. This impacts the quality of care, the amount of testing, and the working environment. So doctors and nurses practice medicine with an eye over their shoulders about whether they might get sued if something goes wrong and whether the procedures they think should be done will actually be available. This combination places hurdles between the doctor and the patient that affect both the cost of care and quality of care.

That being said, even though the threat of malpractice constantly hovers over caregivers, malpractice awards only drive up medical care costs by about 1 percent.[8] The real factors that create the expense lie elsewhere.

Two factors are said to make our health care system so expensive: (1) the way we *manage* that care, and (2) *who* and *what* determines what care is paid for.[9]

The first cause is that we have chosen to allow insurers to manage our care, and that means that the marketing, underwriting, administration, and profit of the insurer all significantly impact the cost of care. Estimates are that 20 cents of every insurance dollar does not pay for medical care. By analogy, most missionary organizations apply a 10 to 12 percent charge to cover administrative fees for the missionaries they manage.[10] No other country structures their medical care so that insurers—who are certainly not a disinterested party—are allowed to make life-and-death decisions for those they insure. Interestingly, the government's fee for the administration of Medicare is only about 3 percent, and the British system operates at a 5 percent level.

> No other country structures their medical care so that insurers—who are certainly not a disinterested party—are allowed to make life-and-death decisions for those they insure.

Until Obamacare, the United States was also unique in allowing insurers to decide *who* gets covered. The situation allowed insurers to reject people who changed jobs and had pre-existing conditions. In a system where insurers are primarily concerned about profits, paying out on expensive patients does not serve their bottom line. It also puts pressure on people seeking consistent preventive care before they get sick, a strategy doctors argue is an important part of medical care. What becomes expensive is when doctors are forced to oversee and gain approval for medical decisions they deem important but that are not approved by the insurance company. Fully 30 percent of medical claims are initially refused in this country. In other countries, if the doctor requests the procedure, it will be done. Even though many of these refusals are reversed on appeal, the time and energy expended to get there is expensive. The ethical questions about profit versus care are part of the tangle we have created for ourselves.

The second cause of high expenses is *who* and *what* determines what is paid for and what is not. In considering *who* determines our health care, if all we do is transfer what insurance companies do to the government, we have not really accomplished anything. If instead of insurers, the government decides what is coverable or treatable and who should treat the patient, then the doctor-patient relationship is still hindered.

In considering the *what* of how health care costs are determined, we must review the tables and predetermined rules that often determine how much individuals pay for procedures—depending on factors like age and status. Payment schedules for identical procedures vary widely. And these schedules are tied to the kind of plan a person is on. The same procedure can have ten different prices. All of this takes people to manage how much each procedure costs and who pays what—the insurer or the patient. Issues of long wait lists and other such snafus, as we recently saw at VA hospitals, do not represent a step forward. Whatever health care emerges, most agree that it needs to allow the doctor-patient relationship to be the key factor in how the patient receives care.

Our discussion about what makes our health care so expensive relates to how care has been managed *without* government involved. Frankly, it's a tangled mess. Even with the changes Obamacare has instituted, one issue has not been dealt with—namely, how insurers handle our health care.

Most health care debate in our country has been about "socialized" health care versus privatized insurance. That is not the debate I seek to cover here. My goal is to point out that placing our current approach under either option still leaves us with an expensive program.

Required: A Different Discussion

In our oversimplified world of sound bites, health care has been reduced to a yes or no on government management versus privatized insurance. Simply put, that is not the only conversation and may be the wrong debate.

One way or another, we have to ask how we have managed to complicate our health care system to the extent that it has become too bureaucratic, expensive, and unmanageable. We will have to consider how to untangle the mess we've gotten ourselves into, especially when so many interest groups have such a large stake in the results.

I am a theologian. I am not a doctor, lawyer, insurer, or legislator. With no expertise in the details of these interrelationships, I have no concrete ideas about how to fix what has been described. I have simply presented the biblical and moral values that tell me we can and should do better in seeking the common good and caring for one another. Basic human and moral concerns should drive our discussion more than they do.

The facts and factors I have presented tell me that a different kind of conversation is needed—one that considers how to adjust what we are currently doing. Most would agree that we need to shift to a system that is less cumbersome and unwieldy and more compassionate. The needed discussion is not simply about the government; it cannot ignore the roles the different industries play in our health care system, as well as issues of affordability. But the discussion needs to be a hard look at how to improve the direct line that should exist between a doctor and patient. Caregivers who serve the well-being and preservation of human life should be allowed to do their job.

CONTROVERSIAL COVERAGE MANDATES

Our form of comprehensive health care had and has built-in mandates regarding what employers must cover on behalf of their employees. Aspects of these mandates have been controversial because they have required employers to underwrite access to care that particular institutions or corporations consider a violation of religious conscience. The original legislation gave only churches, synagogues, and mosques religious liberty protection. Schools dedicated to religious values had to provide the comprehensive coverage the law mandated unless they applied for some type of accommodation. That key distinction still exists even as the government has made adjustments. These accommodations have been and are controversial because access to religious liberty was not assumed, but had to be approved by the government. Particularly sensitive here are choices tied to birth control, the morning-after pill, and even IUDs. These medicines and devices lead to what some regard as abortion.[11] We will look at the issue of abortion later on, but an element of the conversation fits here.

For some long-standing religious traditions, including Roman Catholicism, any form of birth control is a violation of religious conscience. Different traditions and individuals have different views on where to draw the moral line when it comes to contraception and the use of a variety of birth control devices. In addition, the rights of people to gain access to certain procedures tied to abortion or morning-after pills clash with the religious conscience of those sharing in the underwriting of that care. What makes this even more challenging are the steep fines tied to not providing such care.

This legal and moral dilemma is winding its way through

the courts. The government had made a threefold distinction in handling such cases until the recent Hobby Lobby case.

First, as already noted, the government had offered an exemption from providing such care to synagogues, churches, and other institutions that are directly engaged in what is deemed religious activity (houses of worship). This now includes churches where non-followers are employed; but in the original proposal such hiring disqualified a house of worship from the exemption. The government had taken the position that those institutions are covered by freedom of religion and religious conscience, but the nature of the government's current ruling probably reserves the right of the government to change its mind again on this.

The current ruling, pending a court decision in 2016, also mandates that the institution in question provide instruction to employees on what they were not providing. The purchased plan still has to cover the charges, but the religious organization is not "charged" for the service. The original argument was that they were not providing the service. But how does that all make sense? Will not the insurer of that plan build in the anticipated costs? In other words, the system still encourages the availability of something these religious institutions do not regard as moral, and they have to pay into a plan that provides the controversial service.[12] Any other religious organizations or businesses, such as religious colleges or privately owned businesses run by people with such beliefs, did not have direct access to this exclusion and originally were mandated to provide such care.

Second, the government postponed punitive action on religious schools and other religious-oriented organizations that did not comply. Many of these issues are still in the courts, though the Hobby Lobby case was decided in favor of the religious conscience of certain types of privately held businesses.

The distinction is between *houses of worship* and *religious institutions* that the government regards as tangential to religion—even if their activity is completely religious. This means that religious schools, seminaries, and colleges are not exempt and could one day be required to cover such procedures if they lose their challenges in the courts or if the government changes its mind on giving accommodations. With court cases and appeals in process regarding groups such as Little Sisters of the Poor and Wheaton College, providing such care is still currently required.

I am on the board of such a school and have served on a task force for that board, which is involved in litigation to challenge the decision not to accommodate Christian colleges.

As in many such controversial issues, the question is not that simple. When one person's rights lead to the violation of another person's rights, things get complicated. So again the issue is one of balancing the choices and hearing both sides of the question: religious liberty of institutions that provide care versus the provision of certain services an individual might desire.

When one person's rights lead to the violation of another person's rights, things get complicated.

As already noted, the *third* level of distinction provided no accommodation at all for for-profit organizations that were predominantly owned by people who object on religious and moral grounds to providing such services for their employees. Such entities originally were required to provide these services, as of mid-2014, and were subject to the fines failure to comply mandated. But when Hobby Lobby sued to reverse this governmental claim and won a narrow 5–4 decision in its favor, these groups received better than an accommodation, they received a clean exemption. The grounds were religious liberty, on the basis of being a business owned by a person or persons whose religious beliefs prohibited certain procedures.

In situations like the one of Hobby Lobby, the same two conflicting ideas are at play as with religious institutions: the individual's right to and choice about care versus the religious and moral views of the one buying the insurance. The original law forced providers to pay for care that they viewed as immoral—thus, a violation of their conscience.[13]

But now it seems we are headed in the direction of compromise. Objectionable procedures could be pooled into a generic plan for the population and underwritten at large by the government so that individuals can opt in for the procedure and receive their personally desired care. At the same time, the employer is not forced to cover something directly or indirectly that they find morally objectionable. In this way rights on both sides can be respected. However, we are not quite there yet.

Where things stand at this point is that the government has adjusted the accommodation, forms, and method of communication in a way that claims to shield the organization from direct connection to anything the insurer does. The most the school or other organization has to do is to tell employees the name of the company that covers them so individuals can work with that insurance company to get the desired care. This way, the responsibility for providing the care is said to shift from the organization to the insurer. What this means is that those who argue that certain procedures are immoral are not forced to pay directly for their employees' choices, while the person who chooses to utilize such procedures is both covered and has access to them.

The moral choice and the responsibility for that choice lies solely with that person. This plan is almost a good example of the kind of compromise that strives for the "common good" in a widely pluralistic context, even if each side does not get all it originally sought. And it serves to free up gridlock—an end goal that most everyone wants. Still the problem remains that the school's plan must provide the care. So the school is not as entirely disentangled from the care as is claimed. For some, that still means moral responsibility and involvement, so they object.

A clean fix would be to detach the cost and the program that provides these morally debated services from a school's specific plan. No "accommodation" need be required, but simply an identification that a school has a moral objection—much as a conscientious objector can get out of certain types of military service.[14] This structure may seem a bit complicated, but it does communicate respect for our diversity in areas of historic moral disagreement. It also protects one of the most unique and treasured features of American governance enshrined in our First Amendment: the issue of religious freedom. It is a feasible way of balancing competing rights, concerns, and views.

PROTECTING BOTH RELIGIOUS FREEDOM AND FREEDOM FROM RELIGION

Religious freedom itself has become a contentious concept. It was established because the framers appreciated the role of religious reflection in the public square, as documented in the early chapters of this book. It was a way of protecting the original diversity that formed our country. To have discourse about our mutual accountability to a presence greater than all of us not only reflects where most in the world are, but—when properly applied—forces us to consider what our humanness asks of us outside of selfish considerations.

Religious freedom protects not one religion, but all religions, including no religion. It recognizes that much of the world and the people who have come here from other countries possess a variety of faith beliefs about God. By not privileging any one worldview, religious freedom allows us to live well, despite our differences. Religious freedom also honors the individual's choice to relate to the creation however he or she sees fit. Religious freedom is not confined to what happens within a church, synagogue, or mosque's walls, but is also applicable in the actions of the believer—of whatever faith and wherever he or she is.

As such, religious freedom also protects freedom of conscience in a place where consciences differ. It prohibits the establishment of any one faith as the faith of the country and also allows for no faith. So it affirms the role of the heart in our interactions. Religious freedom's presence, including the right to be free from religion, suggests the wisdom of a structure that says we must live together with these differences. It also suggests that the government does not have the right to force me to violate my heart and soul. It is a value worth protecting because it guards all of us from a potential subtle threat of corporate tyranny.[15]

SO . . . WHAT WOULD JESUS SAY ABOUT HEALTH CARE?

Probably the most foundational biblical truth on this topic is the astounding value that God places on human life. As we review the biblical teachings next, we get a clear picture of Jesus' priorities in dealing with people in need.

- *Our value is based on God's love for us:* Because we are *all* created in the image of God, we have inherent value (Genesis 1:27). As we make decisions about how to care for the people of our country, the value of human life must direct our decisions.

- *Compassion leads to helping:* In Matthew 14:13–14, Jesus looked out on a large crowd that had invaded his rare quiet time and *"had compassion on them and healed their sick."* We see Jesus' compassion throughout his ministry. As we imitate him, our compassion will move us to help.

- *A person's financial status has nothing to do with our responsibility to care for him or her:* As we form our ideas regarding caring for others, we must consider the advantage of the wealthy over the poor. The book of James speaks to the distinctions we often make (James 2:1–4 NIV): *"[You] must not show favoritism. Suppose a man comes into your meeting wearing a gold ring and fine clothes, and a poor man in filthy old clothes also comes in. If you show special attention to the man wearing fine clothes . . . have you not discriminated among yourselves and become judges?"*

- *Well wishes without action are futile:* Sometimes, we do feel a tug of sympathy for someone in need of care, but here's what the Bible says about sympathy without action (James 2:15–16): *"If a brother or sister is poorly clothed and lacks daily food, and one of you says to them, 'Go in peace, keep warm and eat well,' but you do not give them what the body needs, what good is it?'"*

Health care is complicated, but the idea that access to medical care should be open to anyone reflects the core moral principles that life is precious and that we should be concerned for our neighbor.

Because core human needs are involved, this cannot be a strictly market-driven decision. If we choose to follow Jesus, we must seek to care for one another.

As with every topic in this book, meaningful conversation is a must. Our task is to balance all the factors that could make for more efficient care, while underscoring our decisions with unbiased compassion.

HISPANIC IMMIGRATION to the United States is a complex phenomenon. It has a history that extends back over 160 years. The history is not only about the movement of people across borders; it is also the story of complicated legislation and diverse cultural reactions. The number of immigrants, documented and undocumented, who have entered the country over the past thirty years has made this phenomenon the focus of national debate at many levels and in all sorts of arenas. The debate has been heated, and it has generated interesting alliances that cross traditional ideological lines. Those who favor more restrictive immigration policy are nativists, environmentalists, low-skilled laborers who feel threatened, some unions, and citizens fearful about national security, the economic viability of social services, and the future of reigning cultural identity. Those who favor a more open strategy include free market thinkers, business and agricultural interests, the AFL–CIO, human rights organizations and activists, and much of academia. Strange bedfellows indeed!

—M. DANIEL CARROLL-RODAS, *CHRISTIANS AT THE BORDER: IMMIGRATION, CHURCH & THE BIBLE*

6

Immigration

The Character of a Society

IMMIGRATION IS another hotly contested issue, as the quotation on the opposite page suggests. That quote focuses on Hispanic immigration, which contributes a unique element to the overall discussion, but the entry into the country is bigger than one group. Realizing that the different groups who want to be a part of the United States have different reasons for coming here prevents us from generalizations about why certain things should or should not be done.

The issue of immigration does not fall along normal ideological lines. Rather than being about big or little government, it's about the character of a society. While both sides share legitimate concerns, the competing positions that inform this debate have led to gridlock. Most recognize that the current system, much like health care, is broken; but the way to fix the immigration issue and the sequence of proposed steps are up for grabs.

The first factor in this tension involves the right of a nation to control her borders and to decide how and whom to incorporate into America. America's reputation as a place of limitless opportunity is best pictured by the Statue of Liberty. This gift from France, given to the United States more than a century ago, was said to symbolize the freedom and opportunity the nation offered to many coming from overseas, especially from Europe. No one who has been to Ellis Island in New York City, where boats with immigrants passed the statue upon entry, can fail to appreciate what our generous immigration policy has meant for our country. Most of us are here because America welcomed our ancestors.

The second factor is a strange combination of invitation, opportunity-seeking, and eye-winking that often encouraged people to come and establish themselves—all without careful enforcement of the policy the government put into place several decades ago. The fact that the most recent policy has existed for around thirty years means that several generations of undocumented and illegal people have been and are here, often with our initial acceptance. This has created an internal social challenge that all recognize as needing adjustments.

Biblical values stand on both ends of this conversation. The result is another complicated debate where cherry-picking on one side or the other ignores key human and societal factors in play. We'll begin with a consideration of the biblical values at work and then consider the ethics of the issue.

Cherry-picking on one side or the other ignores key human and societal factors in play.

WHAT THE BIBLE SAYS ABOUT OUR RESPONSIBILITY TO THE NEEDY AND THE FOREIGNER

I live in Texas. Immigration is a particularly sensitive topic here. Cities like San Antonio, Houston, and Dallas have significant Hispanic populations. Houston is the most diverse city in the country, where distinct sections of the city have a concentration of particular ethnicities. For example, our seminary extension in Houston is located in a part of the city known as Little India. Tex-Mex is everywhere and is a popular feature of cultural dining. I once led a men's Bible study on the topic of immigration, and because of the topic's sensitivity, I handled it differently than any study I've conducted in more than forty years of teaching the Bible.

I opened the study by asking everyone in the room where their family came from and how long ago. Of the twenty-five or so attending, all but two knew their family histories. Most of them had been here four or five generations, largely reflecting the influx of Europeans in the latter part of the nineteenth and early part of the twentieth centuries. We all were beneficiaries of the "bring me your tired, poor, and hungry" call that led many here.

I listed about a dozen texts that addressed the twin themes of respect for government and what God says about caring for the needy and the foreigner. Then I had them read one passage at a time, without intervening comment. The idea was not to discuss immigration until all the texts had been read out loud and all the biblical elements were on the table. What followed was a frank but balanced conversation wrestling with the factors we are about to examine. As our Bible study group saw, and as we'll see in this chapter, the Old Testament commands to care for the needy and the foreigner were taught to the Israelites as a way to apply their own experience as slaves in Egypt, where they were treated very poorly. They were to use their experiences to determine how to respond to others. The format of that class changed the discussion to the degree that we turned our attention from immigration, per se, and focused on how to balance all the factors biblical values raised.

In the following texts, the word under discussion can be translated either as *foreigner* or *alien*. I've chosen to translate it as *alien* to make it clear that it references an outsider.

The New Testament

For those who favor a more restrictive immigration policy, Romans 13:1–7 is the key text. Verses 1–2 say this: *"Let every person be subject to the governing authorities. For there is no authority except by God's appointment, and the authorities that exist have been instituted by God. So the person who resists such authority resists the ordinance of God, and those who resist will incur judgment."* Here, we are directly told to be subject to those who govern us and to recognize their authority as from God.

We do see examples of civil disobedience in Scripture, but usually with a willingness to pay the consequences of the act. Daniel in the Old Testament and the Apostles in Acts 3–4 come to mind. Acts 3 and 4—where Peter and John choose to defy the Jewish authorities and continue to preach—often is the linchpin used to justify a more restrictive policy. The argument is that just as Peter and John had to live with the consequences of the choice to disobey, when immigrants violate immigration law, they, too, are subject to the consequences. End of discussion. The argument also contends that it is unjust to allow any accommodation to that fact. The key defense put forward for this point of view is that we are a nation of the rule of law. The affirmation makes a fair point, but we have to ask: Is this issue really that simple biblically?

It is far too easy to simply claim that those who want to place heavier restrictions on immigrants are either racist or long for an America where the realities of globalization and pluralism are not being realistically faced. As the recent debates in the 2016 presidential campaign have shown, there are legitimate concerns about national security and terrorism, as well as the criminal, drug, and sexual violence that an open policy leaves us exposed to as a society. So concern for law and order applies a societal value for our overall well-being.

Exodus, Numbers, and Deuteronomy

Those who are for a more open policy emphasize a series of texts that speak about how the alien, or foreigner, should be treated. It is a rich theme with several passages.

- Exodus 23:9 reads, *"Do not oppress an alien; you yourselves know how it feels to be aliens, because you were aliens in Egypt."* (NIV)
- Similar is Leviticus 19:34: *"You shall love the alien as yourself, for you were aliens in Egypt."* (Author's translation.)
- Exodus 22:21 reads, *"Do not mistreat or oppress an alien, for you were an alien in Egypt."* (Author's translation.)
- Deuteronomy 10:19 says the same kind of thing, using the refrain *"for you were aliens in the land of Egypt."* This empathy was meant to drive how the Israelites saw and treated those from the outside.
- Numbers 15:15 says, *"The community is to have the same rules for you and for the alien living among you; this is a*

lasting ordinance for generations to come." (Author's translation.)
- Similar are Exodus 12:49 and Leviticus 24:22.

Proverbs and the Prophets
The theme continues like a chorus in the Proverbs and Prophets.

- Proverbs 31:9 sings, *"Defend the rights of the poor and the needy."* (ESV)
- In Micah 6:8 (NET), justice is combined with compassion in what is a key text. It reads, *"He has told you, O man, what is good, and what the LORD really wants from you: He wants you to promote justice, to be faithful, and to live obediently before your God."*
- Zechariah 7:9–10 echoes the call of Micah 6:8 to promote justice and teaches, *"The LORD who rules over all said, 'Exercise true judgment and show brotherhood and compassion to each other. You must not oppress the widow, the orphan, the alien, or the poor, nor should anyone secretly plot evil against his fellow human being.'"* (Author's translation.) Tim Keller cites Nicholas Wolterstorff who has called these four groups—the widow, the orphan, the alien, and the poor—the "quartet of the vulnerable."[1] Justice is about giving people their due. It aims to do what is right.

Jesus
Now we add to all the above a text in Luke 10:25–37 where a lawyer asks Jesus, *"Who is my neighbor?"* The lawyer asks this in an effort to limit his responsibility by suggesting that certain people might not be his neighbors. Jesus responds by

telling the story of a Samaritan who loved well and without ethnic concern, a man who modeled compassion and concern to another who had fallen among robbers. When Jesus asks the lawyer which man was a neighbor, the lawyer would not even acknowledge that the compassionate man was a Samaritan and simply describes him as one who had mercy. Jesus tells the lawyer, *"Go and do the same"* (v. 37). Jesus calls us here to seek what is humane and to do that. He tells us this is how to be a good neighbor and that neighbors can come in surprising packages.

REFLECTING GOD'S IMAGE

Scripture has God unashamedly pleading for the poor and the foreigner, the widow and the orphan. Biblical values emphatically and repeatedly say we should do the same. This moral value echoes back to the fact that we are all made in the image of God (Genesis 1). Psalm 146:7–9 portrays attributes of our Creator that we are to emulate as we reflect his image. Here is its note of praise to God about his actions: *"He executes justice for the oppressed and gives food to the hungry. The Lord sets prisoners free, the Lord gives sight to the blind, he lifts up those who are bowed down, the Lord loves those who live justly. The Lord watches over the immigrant and sustains the fatherless and the widow, but he frustrates the ways of the wicked"* (author's translation).[2] The role of the delivering Servant of God in Isaiah 61:1–2 echoes this passage. This Isaiah passage is one Jesus cites as reflective of his own mission in Luke 4:18–19. Jesus has come *"to preach good news to the poor, to proclaim forgiveness to the captives and give sight to the blind, and to set free the oppressed"* (author's translation).

Deuteronomy 10:17–19 continues the theme: "*The Lord your God . . . defends the cause of the fatherless and the widow, and loves the alien giving him food and clothing. So show your love for the alien*" (author's translation). When we put all of these texts on the table, we see the real and legitimate tension between obeying the government and treating everyone with fairness, compassion, and humanitarian justice. And yet there is a repeated—even emphasized—biblical concern that we are to especially show sensitivity to those who are from another place. How we care and show that care is a core moral value of Scripture. It is a reflection of a people's character.

Scripture has God unashamedly pleading for the poor
and the foreigner, the widow and the orphan.

Deuteronomy 27:19 warns, "*Cursed be anyone who withholds the justice due to the immigrant, the fatherless, and the widow. Then all the people shall say, 'Amen!'*"[3] (author's translation).

Justice is not just about meting out punishment. It is about pursuing and doing what is right, including at a humanitarian level. It allows for and calls for self-correction, even at a corporate level. So perhaps we need to reconsider how we treat those from outside our country.

How We Got Here: The History of Immigration

I opened the chapter with a remark about the Statue of Liberty and Ellis Island. We have always romanticized this period in our recent past. Immigration has been a kind of dance for Americans—a love-hate relationship.

To begin our thinking about the history of immigration, let's remember Ellis Island.[4] At Ellis Island and other sites like it, people came over on a boat with no papers or visa, and they were able to apply for and receive status within hours. This is how many of our ancestors got into the USA. But times have changed and so has access, as well as enforcement. And so now we are left with a broken approach—an approach that needs fixing and adjustment. Let's take a brief look at the history of immigration to give us some context of how things began, how we got here, and where we are.

1751: Even before there was a United States, there was debate about immigration. In 1751, Benjamin Franklin complained about the influx of Germans into Pennsylvania impacting the homogeneous character of that state. It was a fear of the influx of a distinct culture that raised the concern. Yet who would complain about the impact of German culture on our country now? Franklin's fear of the arrival of others is opposite of the verse, written in 1883, by Emma Lazarus. These poetic lines sit with the Statue of Liberty: "Give me your tired, your poor, your huddled masses yearning to breathe free, the wretched refuse of your teeming shore. Send these, the homeless, temptest-tost to me, I lift my lamp beside the golden door!" The words are a symbolic beacon of American values that affirm the desire of people to come here.

1840s: During this period, the potato famine in Ireland brought many Irish to America, and the revolution in German states brought many Germans. In just one day, the Treaty of Guadalupe Hidalgo in 1848 proclaimed 100,000 people to be citizens, as the United States had acquired what became California and several other Western states extending to New Mexico.

Thousands of Mexicans became legal Americans on that day, a reminder that many Mexican-Americans have been here a long time, legally, for several generations. Also throughout much of this period until the Civil War, many Africans were stolen from their homes and brought to America to work as slaves. That is a darker side to this story.

1882: Immigration debates have always been with us. In 1882, the government passed the Chinese Exclusion Act. It was the first restrictive legislation regarding immigration. Virtually no Chinese were allowed into the country for more than sixty years, until the Exclusion Act was repealed in 1943. Along with the Chinese Exclusion Act, other restrictions were applied to people who were unable to care for themselves. This reversed a previous policy that allowed anyone in, provided they held promise of being a good citizen and employable.

1880–1920: During this period, Southern and Eastern Europeans flooded into places like Ellis Island. This is when both sides of my family arrived in the United States. More than 23 million immigrated during this time. Italians and Russians, among others, were numerous. Now that these people have been well assimilated into our society, who would complain about their presence as a part of our national fabric? Their assimilation shows what is possible.

During this same time period, things were different on the West Coast, at Angel Island in San Francisco Bay. There was much suspicion of Asians, so existing facilities were utilized to detain them. People were held for long periods of time, as decisions were made about whether to let them in or turn them away. Some people were held for as long as six months.

1917: Renewed concerns about race and culture led to more restrictions in 1917, when literacy requirements were added for all immigrants, which effectively excluded most Asians.

1924–65: In 1924, a quota system was intensified to control immigration through the Immigration Act of 1924, also known as the Johnson-Reed Act. With that law, the number of people who could enter the country was calculated as only 2 percent of the US population, versus an earlier 3 percent. Even though a census was taken in 1920, calculations were made from the smaller national population numbers of 1890. The purpose and effect of this law was to limit the influx to a trickle of what it had been. Only 180,000 immigrants could enter per year.

This law was favorable to the English, the French, and the Germans, but not to other Europeans or to Asians. Southern and Eastern Europeans along with Asians and Africans were the law's main targets. This discrimination cut immigration in half, with some countries' immigration reduced by as much as 90 percent.[5] An exemption was granted for those in the Western Hemisphere, so Canadians and Mexicans were allowed in. Part of the motivation behind the exemption was that Western states wanted Mexican labor.

This law also introduced the idea of visas, shifting our policy from giving access to citizenship to controlling entrance. Most of our ancestors entered the country by simply showing up—similar to how many enter it today, but with one major difference: the old way in was legal and the new way in was and is not.

1942–1964: During this time, Mexico and the US continued with a special program. Each year, up to 400,000 Mexicans entered legally.

1965: But in 1965, the law changed as requirements shifted from national quotas and ethnic concerns to family connections and job skills. The new policy sought to allow families to unite. The goal was still to control entry, but not to have ethnic preferences. The result was that many more came to the United States from Asia, Africa, and outside of Europe. Changes in the

1980s, which is where our laws today come from, did little to alter the 1965 baseline.

TODAY'S RESULTS OF OUR LONG HISTORY

The estimates are that, today, 11 to 12 million immigrants of all ethnicities are here illegally, but what the previous paragraphs also explain is how some 52 million Hispanics—the largest ethnic minority in America—live here legally. Our country contains a mixture of numerous people of other ethnicities who are here legally and seek to bring their families here as well. Those who are illegal are often encouraged to come by family, protected for the most part by those who hire them for their cheaper labor or for their willingness to do jobs others do not want to perform. These illegal immigrants live in a world where enforcement alternates between lenience, looking the other way, and moments of crackdown. Most of us know, and have even benefited from, people working here who are known to be undocumented. The moral responsibility for the situation is a shared one.

These illegal immigrants live in a world where enforcement alternates between lenience, looking the other way, and moments of crackdown.

Moreover, once someone is in the United States—sometimes initially quite legally because of a travel visa or a student visa—there is no clear way *from within* our country for that person to apply to extend his or her visa, since gaining a green card is difficult. Many who enter legally have no real hope of remaining legally, unlike those who came to Ellis Island. So they choose to become illegal and go underground in order to extend their stay. This is a bad choice that is facilitated by a desire to stay, by a poor enforcement policy that allows them to disappear, and by our not having created a solid and efficient means for them to stay and move toward citizenship, if desired. The estimate is that almost half of those who are currently undocumented are here under those circumstances. The result has been that the United States, understandably, has become reluctant to grant visitor visas to people from countries who have made a habit of overstaying.

A cycle has resulted. People from certain countries who wish to gain a green card to prolong their stay and move toward citizenship have difficulty because the United States fears they will simply disappear. This fear is based on their home nation's past record. So there is no way forward for proving themselves worthy of citizenship, even though their skills, intentions, and goals may have allowed them to stay had they been from another country and their presence as good citizens would have benefited us all.

The system, through a variety of complex causes, has become arbitrary and racially imbalanced. Nothing illustrates this more than the variations on the wait to bring family members into the country legally. For a foreign spouse of an American, the wait is basically the paperwork time: six months to two years. For a lawful permanent resident from Canada, it takes five years. For an unmarried child of a US citizen from Mexico, the wait is sixteen years. The wait is the same if that person is a lawful permanent resident from Mexico. If one comes from Iran, the wait is nine years. For an unmarried child of a US citizen from Italy, the wait is six years, while someone from the

Philippines must wait seventeen years. So Western Europeans often get preference with these visas, while those from other countries have far more difficulty. Is this kind of variation just? Is this partiality what the Bible teaches?

Given that this is how things have worked for almost thirty years, we now have some families here with undocumented (grand)parents but children who are legal.[6] In some cases these families have been here for three generations, with a mix of legal and illegal persons.

The pressure of this combination of factors and history has led to the immigration debate we now have. As with health care, there is a disconnect between how our system works and what is humane and just—especially when we consider that the situation has evolved into a full societal problem.

Virtually everyone agrees that the status quo is not working and that something should and must be done. The biblical values cited earlier in this chapter demonstrate that our current approach is problematic, as are any one-sided solutions.

Reducing this discussion to debates about amnesty, usually raised with a negative connotation, vastly oversimplifies how we got into this situation and how we will get out of it. Deportation as the only sanction would split families, separating children from parents in ways that are not humane or moral.[7] It is ironic that some Christians, who say they are pro-family, would want an immigration policy that rips families apart.

Most agree that those who are here illegally or are undocumented should suffer some form of sanction, including a longer time to complete the process. Yet how do we respect the law while producing a more humane system? How do we balance all the biblical and moral elements involved? Cherry-picking one side or the other seems fraught with problems. So where do we go from here?

BUT WHAT ABOUT THE REFUGEES?

The immigration discussion has become more complicated in the last few years by the rise of refugees out of Syria and the Middle East. The problem of refugees, most of them fleeing from the carnage in the area, has become a major issue for Europe as well as for other Western countries.

Many who flee are trying to escape the atrocities inflicted by the same terrorists we fear. It is important to remember that terrorism is a function of radical Islam and is not condoned by most Muslims. Generalizing about a particular religion is inaccurate and problematic. It also obscures the fact that many who are leaving are doing so because they are questioning the religious world that has propelled them to leave. These refugees have to be pretty desperate to pull up all roots and head elsewhere, taking only what they can carry with them to a place that is very different from where they've lived—not even knowing the language of the place they are going.

What most people do not know is that countries like Lebanon have absorbed amazing numbers of these refugees in ways that strain their capability to manage. These refugees live in very basic conditions that most people would not tolerate over a long period of time. So both the refugees and the countries currently taking care of them need real help. In Lebanon, every fifth person is a refugee. If 64 million Mexicans suddenly crossed over the US border, that is the equivalent of what has taken place in Lebanon.[8] There are also accounts of unprecedented openness to exploring different faiths from many who have fled. I have received regular reports from people working both in Lebanon and in places like Albania, where refuges have come to embrace Christianity and left Islam because of their past experiences. On the other hand, the German experience with Turkish folks shows that assimilation is difficult for both the immigrant and the host nation in a society whose roots are so distinct.

Most who are fleeing are seeking genuine refuge and a new life free from the violence, but of course the real possibility exists that some will take advantage of the compassionate reception in order to infiltrate and gain access that otherwise would be prohibited—and to do so for sinister reasons. So although this refugee problem is related to the immigration issue, it is a distinct problem with unique dimensions.

Most who are fleeing are seeking genuine refuge, but of course the real possibility exists that some will take advantage of the compassionate reception.

Clearly, there is both a vast human problem and a security one as well. It is here that the security concerns versus compassion issues run most headlong into each other. These concerns will require careful discussion and development of policy that is able to sort through legitimate asylum and humanitarian requests versus those with sinister intentions. This policy will require careful vetting, even more than currently exists, that prevents prospective terrorists from entering the country. The human and humanitarian problems, as well as the security problem, are so immense that no "all or nothing" policy from either side of the immigration divide is workable, humane, and secure. This particular refugee problem is so complex, it should be seen as a distinct part of the immigration discussion, but it should be pursued with both sets of legitimate concerns very much in view. This is no sound bite issue. It will take careful work and cooperation to craft a position that (1) seeks to be humane, (2) gives a new life to those who have been displaced through no fault of their own, and (3) protects all of us from those who would take advantage of that goodwill for which America and the West are often known.

A Way Forward

The dance of our history shows that the tune we have played as a nation has shifted back and forth between openness and restriction. Our laws have been a moving target mixed with selective enforcement and imbalances that have created the societal pressures we now face. Nothing prevents us from reassessing where we are and considering how we might create a better, more balanced policy for the common good and with an eye to compassion. We have done it before. We can do it again. The question is how. It is a discussion worth having in a serious, sincere, and calm manner—unlike the tone that often accompanies this deliberation, where each side digs in.

A key question in this discussion is whether or not to *sequence* our approach. Should we sequence by fixing the border first and then talking about opportunity for citizenship? Or should we *decouple* the two discussions and work on both simultaneously?

Sequencing

The logic of sequencing is to tighten and enforce illegal-entry restrictions, including deportation, and to step up internal enforcement. Only after those are completed should we look at other issues.[9] The effect of sequencing is to prolong or exacerbate the internal issues that are a key part of the problem. Strict deportation, especially for those who have been here for some time, separates families in ways that are not necessary and are needlessly punitive.

So a sequence that begins with border tightening, tighter enforcement of penalties, and then moves to an internal review means we will go nowhere on this issue for some time, and we will inflict human damage in the process. Sequencing also provides an excuse for those who really don't want change, as they can claim that the borders are not yet fixed so we cannot move on to phase two.

An opposite sequence could be to first work on the internal issues tied to undocumented illegals and our immigration policy questions, and then tackle the border questions. But this approach would continue to allow the flow of undocumented people into our country and would allow security risks to continue. In short, sequencing will not work.

Decoupling

Or, as some have suggested, we could decouple the moral and practical human issues and work on both fronts simultaneously. Deciding how tight to make the entry rules and how to gear up enforcement of those rules will take time. Some have suggested a plan something like this:

1. First, set a date for establishing and enforcing whatever new policy is decided upon.
2. Provide a pathway for people with student or travel visas to extend their visas from within the country and get in line to be citizens.
3. Then set a date to open the queue for citizenship and place those here illegally at the back of that line. This would re-

quire a registration process to start the time line. Penalties for having been illegal will lead to a longer path to citizenship, a way to honor the law.

4. Set quotas that are realistic and generous for those who show they will contribute.

In this way we can start the process that allows people who have lived here without incident to move toward citizenship.

Those who think decoupling is the best way forward argue that it would allow us to get the timer going, allow for a more effective policy, remove the incentive to live underground, work on a coordinated effort on both ends, and help our country financially as new citizens begin to pay their share. Failure to register would be a cause for deportation. The incentive would be that registration allows a person to stay and earn his or her citizenship under a revised, more just law that does carry a penalty. No amnesty, just a restart on the policy. A simultaneous approach will allow for a more comprehensive and effective policy.

WHAT ABOUT PREVIOUS ILLEGALITY?

What about men and women who entered our country in violation of our laws? Should they not be deported as our laws allow? Is the decoupled/simultaneous approach simply amnesty, a policy that thumbs its nose at the current laws? These are legitimate concerns that involve moral, social, and legal challenges.

An appropriate penalty for those who are here illegally would be a longer wait to complete the process. In effect, they would pay a fine with time, even as they become registered and pay into benefits they eventually will earn. In this way the law is honored, those who came in legally or who seek to come in legally are also respected, and a penalty is enforced. This approach also recognizes some moral responsibility on our end for having contributed to this situation through a system that encouraged systemic abuse.

This approach recognizes the illegality of undocumented entry. It penalizes those who did not leave when their visas expired with payment for the crime in time, but it does so in a context where forgiveness and compassion drive the process. It paves the way for policies that move closer to the common good. And it makes us mindful of our ancestors' previous welcome into this land of opportunity. The policy reflects our character as a caring and open nation that still recognizes that people see our land as one of opportunity.

This approach . . . penalizes those who did not leave when their visas expired . . . but it does so in a context where forgiveness and compassion drive the process.

This is not suggesting that we completely open our borders or that we grant amnesty to all illegal residents—making them automatic citizens. Rather, it is a plea to evaluate where we are, take a fresh look at our policy, and create a solution that is compassionate and penalizes violators in ways that are responsible to our laws. To this a careful vetting process needs to be added for those now seeking entry to provide the protection current circumstances require.

So . . . What Would Jesus Say about Immigration?

As we review the scriptures laid out in this chapter, we will find a pretty clear picture of where Jesus and Scripture would stand on this issue. By way of reminder, when the Bible uses the term *alien* or *foreigner*, it refers to people from other countries who live among us. Of note, these scriptures are all worded as commands—not as general principles:

- As followers of Christ, we are to submit to governing authority.
- We are emphatically told not to oppress or mistreat the foreigner, or alien.
- One step further . . . we are told to defend the rights of the poor and needy.
- One step even further . . . we are commanded to love the alien.
- We are told that the rules we put on aliens are to be the same ones that we follow. And this emphasis is added by God: *"this is a lasting ordinance for generations to come."*
- People of other nationalities—even nationalities that are hated by many—are our neighbors and we are to care for them. We are to reflect the character of God in the way we treat people from other countries.

If we want to view this issue in light of biblical teaching, then the above commands are mandatory as moral principles. They apply to our attitudes, our hearts, our actions—and in this context, to our political positions.

As with the other issues we have covered, we have seen there are real concerns on each side of this debate. It also is clear that biblical values call us to be sensitive to those who are here from a foreign land. We are urged to be just in our engagement with them, just as biblical values call for a respect for law. With this subject, the way forward involves some knowledge of our past history, awareness of current realities, and facing the tensions that need resolving. This is a better way forward than simply lining up on one side or the other.

What is needed is yet another balanced conversation. The result might just be a policy that operates for the common good and that enriches us by adding depth to the diversity that has shaped this country since its founding.

Every question about guns, gun violence, or gun policy is contentious. Basic facts—the annual number of gun transactions or even the number of guns in private hands—are not known with any precision. Estimates of the costs and consequences of our nation's gun control laws are hotly disputed. Disparate beliefs about whether widespread gun possession is a guarantor of freedom and personal safety, or on the contrary a leading cause of early death and neighborhood decline, fuel acrimonious debates at family gatherings, online, and in the halls of government.

—PHILIP J. COOK AND KRISTIN A. GOSS,
THE GUN DEBATE: WHAT EVERYONE NEEDS TO KNOW

7

Gun Control

Self-Defense or Restraint?

Like health care and immigration, gun control is a hot-button issue. The tension in this issue is the presence of violence, including mass killings, versus the right to protect ourselves and the constitutional right to bear arms. Because human lives are involved, there is much at stake. The impetus behind both sides is the same—concern for human life. Whether we are concerned that guns can be abused as weapons of violence, and thus should be restricted, or we are concerned that our right to protect ourselves and our families is in jeopardy, so we should possess guns, we care about the value of human life. Add to the discussion the recent human tragedies of mass murders in schools and other events, and we can see why the debate is so heated. So how should we think about an issue where each side is arguing that the preservation of life is what they are most concerned about defending?

In the United States—and with the Second Amendment—

the issue is not whether guns can or should be allowed in public. The American discussion is quite different than it is in Europe—where places like the UK have strict gun control and limit access to such weapons. But in America, millions of guns are already here. Since gun registration does not take place in every locale, there is no way to know exactly how many guns are out there. Estimates are that 35 percent of homes and 25 percent of adults own a gun. Many gun owners own multiple weapons, with men outnumbering women by 37 percent to 12 percent. So numbers of guns range from 200 to 300 million.[1] A report notes that we possess three times the amount of firearms per person than the next highest country, which is Canada.[2] Whatever the number is, the reality is that people have and will have guns in the United States, and there are lots of them out there.

DOES THE SCRIPTURE EVEN SPEAK TO THIS?

At one level, this topic postdates the Bible. There were no guns when the Bible was written or when Jesus was alive! So our way into the moral reflection on this topic is to consider how Scripture handles issues like violence and self-defense—two of our key issues today. Once we answer these questions, we have all kinds of directions and complexities to consider.

Our way into the moral reflection on this topic
is to consider how Scripture handles issues like
violence and self-defense.

One issue involves the tension between *pacifism*, or *non-retaliation*, and "just war," or the restrained use of violence in a context of self-defense.

Pacifism and Non-retaliation

The concept of pacifism is bolstered by Jesus' remarks in the Sermon on the Mount.

- Matthew 5:38–42 in part says, *"Do not resist the evildoer. But whoever strikes you on the right cheek, turn the other to him as well. And if someone wants to sue you and to take your tunic, give him your coat also. And if anyone forces you to go one mile, go with him two."*
- Luke 6:27–30 says similarly, *"Love your enemies, do good to those who hate you, bless those who curse you, pray for those who mistreat you. To the person who strikes you on the cheek, offer the other as well, and from the person who takes away your coat, do not withhold your tunic either. Give to everyone who asks you, and do not ask for your possessions back from the person who takes them away."*

Of course, we would all agree that being hit is not the same threat as the risk to your life or the lives of your family by gunfire. But Jesus, in the above passage, does speak to the issue of non-retaliation. More below comes from Paul in the New Testament . . .

- Romans 12:18–19: *"If possible, so far as it depends on you, live peaceably with all people. Do not avenge yourselves, dear friends, but give place to God's wrath, for it is written, 'Vengeance is mine, I will repay,' says the Lord."*

Non-retaliation tells us that vengeance is not ours to seek. When someone wrongs us, Jesus says, we are to accept the wrong and repay it with kindness. Romans adds a note that says we are not to act out of revenge. Some justice only God is to repay.

- The Book of Acts consistently portrays the church as reacting nonviolently when faced with persecution. Most of those persecuted were either martyred or moved away from the violence rather than retaliate. In Acts 3–4, Peter and John do not resist arrest for breaking the law. In Acts 9:25, Paul is lowered in a basket to escape persecution in Damascus. He never is portrayed in Acts as fighting back.

Self-Defense and "Just War"

On the other side of the ledger are texts that point to *self-defense* and that allow for *"just war."* We'll think first about *self-defense.*

- Exodus 22:2 argues that someone who kills a thief in the night is not liable for their action: *"If a thief is caught breaking in and is struck so that he dies, there will be no blood guilt for him"*—meaning, the homeowner will not be guilty for killing the robber.

Interestingly, the next verse says that if someone kills a thief in the day, then he *is* liable for his action. The implication being that we do not have an automatic right to kill the intruder.

- Nehemiah 4:17–18, in speaking about those who were rebuilding the wall of Jerusalem, says: *"Those who were carrying loads did so by keeping one hand on the work and*

the other on their weapon. The builders to a man had their
swords strapped to their sides while they were building." Scripture assumes a person's right to self-defense.

- Romans 13:1–4 speaks of the government having the right to wield the sword: "*Let every person be subject to the governing authorities. . . . Do you desire not to fear authority? Do good and you will receive its commendation, for it is God's servant for your good. But if you do wrong, be in fear, for it does not bear the sword in vain.*"

- Esther 8:11 notes that the Persian king allowed the Jews to defend themselves and their property. "*The king thereby allowed the Jews who were in every city to assemble and to stand up for themselves.*" Self-defense is actually about respect for life and the right to protect it. Such respect for life introduces a tension in that one can defend life, but also one is to be slow to take it.

- In Luke 22:36, Jesus enigmatically told his disciples to buy a sword, but he told them to put away their swords when one of them cut off the ear of the high priest's slave during his arrest in Luke 22:50–51. Jesus' command reflected that he was willing to carry out his calling to die on the cross. So special circumstances may be at work in this example. In the book of Revelation, we see the picture of Jesus going to war—a picture of judgment that assumes a battle to defend what is right and just. "Just war" theory is where war is a last resort and restraint is used when violence is necessary, and the violence is carried out with legitimacy by an appropriate authority. The goal is to establish peace and redress a wrong. The force used is proportional to the need to accomplish success in battle and avoids excessive use of power and the harming of civilians, where possible.

- 1 Samuel 25:32–33: Restraint in the use of violence is praised when Abigail restrains David with regard to sparing her wicked husband Nabal: *"Then David said to Abigail. . . . 'Praised be your good judgment! May you yourself be rewarded for having prevented me this day from shedding blood and taking matters into my own hands!'"*
- Proverbs 3:31 and Psalm 44:6–7: We can add to this list of biblical principles the call not to trust in violence in texts from Proverbs and Psalms. Proverbs 3:31 says, *"Do not envy a violent man, and do not choose to imitate any of his ways,"* and in Psalm 44:6–7 we are told not to trust in the bow or sword.

After looking at the wealth of Scripture that addresses pacifism and non-retaliation—as well as self-defense, "just war," and restrained force—we see that we have several biblical principles to weigh as we consider the use of violence. In sum, the Bible teaches that we have the right to defend but that we are to do so with restraint.

With all these competing factors in play, it seems obvious that room for serious discussion exists.

SO WHAT ABOUT GUN CONTROL?

Complicating the conversation on violence are some surprising statistics on gun control. It is widely believed that reducing access to weapons would drive down the level of crime. It is what I instinctively thought before I began research on this subject. The statistics on this point are somewhat unexpected and mixed.

Among the more famous studies is by John Lott. His book

title says it all: *More Guns, Less Crime: Understanding Crime and Gun Control Laws.* Lott's book is full of statistics that argue that restricting access to guns does not lead to a decrease in crime.[3] Although some have vehemently contested his work, it is not clear that the challenge cancels the data he presents. Interestingly, even a work by Craig Whitney, which advocates more gun control, does not entirely dispute Lott's evidence. Whitney's *Living with Guns: A Liberal's Case for the Second Amendment* argues that "strict gun-control laws by themselves do not lead to less gun violence."[4] Whitney is a former *New York Times* reporter and editor. What these studies may well indicate is that our society has so many guns in circulation already that restrictive laws do little or nothing to curtail their use. In a world where millions of guns already circulate and criminals break the law, restricting additions matters little.

What these studies may well indicate is that our society has so many guns in circulation already that restrictive laws do little or nothing to curtail their use.

As surprising as the Lott data is, it is not the only side of the data discussion. An examination of the state of Missouri's loosening of gun control laws in 2007 has now had several years to allow the collection of statistics and analysis.[5] It shows a rise in violence, especially in more poverty-stricken areas. It is hard to prove direct causation, but the 16 percent rise is troubling and could suggest that looser gun laws have led to the rise, especially in light of the fact than the national rate during the same period showed an 11 percent decline in such violence. From 2008 to 2014, the Missouri rate of violence was 47 percent higher than the national average. Most law enforcement see the loss of background checks as a key element here. So the data on tougher laws and violence is mixed, as the Lott and Missouri examples show. However, careful background checks do not add to the problem and could possibly reduce the opportunity for impulse killings.

Does this mean that we should throw up our hands and simply do the best we can to cope with the amount of weapons already in circulation? After all, some might ask, why put in place restrictions when criminals will seek to circumvent them or get around them anyway? Why make it harder for those who seek to have guns for legal reasons? The question is a fair one; let's consider some possible answers.

Some Proposals for Consideration

Recognizing that guns are a reality in America, issues for genuine discussion remain. Below is the principle Whitney articulated that reflects an attempt to balance the conversation:

> *Effective gun regulation, regulation that has a chance of actually reducing gun violence and crime, has to begin with positive recognition by all Americans who want to achieve it that the right to keep and bear arms is an individual right, and that law-abiding citizens should be able to exercise that right without being made to feel as if they were criminals. But those who value the right must also recognize it is not absolute, and that it comes, as all rights do, with responsibilities. In the beginning, two centuries ago, it was connected to civic duty: militia service in the defense of community and freedom. Today,*

> gun owners should be encouraged to recognize their civic
> duty to do what they can to make the free use of firearms
> safer than it is today—not just for themselves but for all
> of us.[6]

Whitney's is an appeal to recognize some level of common good as a civic duty. Part of achieving this common good is putting reasonable regulation of guns into place. Our rights are already regulated in many areas. A car has to have a license plate, and the driver has to obtain a license to drive it; but that does not cancel our right to drive or our need to show we are able to operate a vehicle, which if misused can do damage. There is no inherent reason that guns should be any different.

In balancing the right of self-defense with the need to curtail the abuse of guns, let's consider together some areas for discussion that fall within the principles already noted. Bringing the biblical principles we've discussed into this conversation about reasonable regulation of rights and the pursuit of the common good leads us to the following proposals.[7, 8]

Proposal One

Ensure that the national instant background check database is appropriately up-to-date with its reporting of drug abusers, the psychologically disturbed, and others already outlawed from being gun purchasers. People in these categories are often the perpetrators of mass killings and also are the victims of almost half the suicides that take place each year.[9] As I write, the country is going through the postmortem on a mass killing in California near UC Santa Barbara. The perpetrator was a deranged young man who decided to go on a rampage of revenge for wrongs he thought society had delivered to him. Despite some signals that we always seem to catch in retrospect, warning signs were missed. Seven innocent people are dead plus the perpertrator. Tightening regulation for those who might use firearms to do harm to others or themselves is a responsible exercise of what otherwise is a right.[10]

Regularly updating our national background database is a state responsibility. When these lists have holes, checking background is not as effective as it could be. We must be diligent in keeping what is already the law functional. To make this workable, discussion of funding is necessary.

Proposal Two

Bring state and federal penalties for gun crimes into conformity with each other, with harsh and consistent prosecution for those who abuse the proper use of and the right to use guns. Laws in Virginia are an example here. They impose serious penalties for abuse of the right to use guns. Harsh penalties can serve as a deterrent and communicate societal concern for a serious violation of public trust. When the state and federal penalties differ greatly, prosecution for the harsher penalty for real crime should be allowed.

Proposal Three

Require background checks for anyone buying a gun anywhere, including gun shows. This would mean closing exemptions that currently exist for some private sellers of arms. California, Rhode Island, and the District of Columbia have such laws already. Background checks would flag for previous firearms abuse, the use of drugs, and mental illness. In some cases of first-time drug violations, the prohibition might exist for a set period and then be withdrawn. These details can be discussed and developed.

Proposal Four

Create a federal firearms trafficking statute that will penalize straw purchasers of guns and gun dealers who knowingly sell to them. A straw purchase occurs when the actual buyer of a firearm cannot pass the required federal background check and does not want his or her full name associated with the purchase—and so has another person who can pass the required background check purchase the firearm. Provided that the "straw" purchaser knew what he or she was doing when passing on the gun, that person would be penalized as an accomplice. Admittedly, it is harder to hold the gun dealer responsible here, so protections would be erected to protect against false prosecution. Still an interesting old statistic that tracked this issue is that 0.5 percent of gun shop owners accounted for more than half the crime guns sold in 1996–98, so something is clearly going on in certain shops.[11] More recent statistics from 2007 show that sixteen out of seventeen gun sales are to people who will sell to a straw purchaser.[12] Such dealers should be held more civically accountable.

Proposal Five

License gun owners the same way those who drive a car or sell alcoholic beverages are licensed. This licensing could be through local or state agencies to show that owners are able to use and store a gun safely. Some states have such laws. Under this proposal, the licensing would be extended across the nation to each state. Hawaii and the District of Columbia already have such laws. This kind of approach goes back to the colonial era when states wanted to document who could or would make up their militia, showing that belief in the right to bear arms did not preclude exercising that right responsibly. This need not be a national registration, as such basic regulation does not require it.

This kind of approach goes back to the colonial era when states wanted to document who could or would make up their militia.

None of these proposals prevents a qualified person from having a weapon. They simply seek to track the weapon's use and monitor the qualifications of those who use it.

AUTOMATIC AND SEMIAUTOMATIC WEAPONS

The last category for discussion is more controversial, since it does raise the issue of arms curtailment. This discussion here is whether we would be wise to ban certain types of weapons from being readily available. Up for discussion are automatic and semiautomatic weapons that can dispense violence more rapidly. The issue here is whether with so many weapons like this already in circulation, such a law, though well intentioned, would actually be able to achieve its goal.

The moral discussion is whether such weapons are really needed for recreation or self-defense, but we must also consider that, practically, we may already be at a point of no return regarding automatic weapons, as we are with guns in general. The reality of our level of gun circulation means that we all must be diligent in our use of the guns we have. Increasing our ability to monitor, trace abuse, and prevent those at risk of misusing guns from gaining easy access are reasonable discussions regarding the use of the right to bear arms.

So ... What Would Jesus Say about Gun Control?

As stated at the beginning of this chapter, there were no guns during the time the Bible was written or when Jesus walked this earth so, of course, we have no direct commands on the topic. But we have plenty of biblical principles to guide our conversation.

Perhaps our best way into this moral discussion is to consider how Scripture handles issues like violence and self-defense—two of our key issues today.

Here's an overview of those principles:

- *Non-retaliation:* Jesus' commands on the topic of non-retaliation are quite stiff. He tells us to turn the other cheek if someone strikes us and to pray for those who mistreat us.
- *Self-defense:* On the other hand, some biblical texts point to self-defense and allow for "just war."
- *Restraint:* The Bible teaches that we have the right to defend but that we are to do so with restraint.
- *Respect for life:* Self-defense is actually about respect for life and the right to protect it. Such respect for life means that we can defend it, but also that we need to be slow to take it.
- *Government authority:* According to Romans, we are to

submit to the authority of the government and the government has the right to use force ("the sword") to enforce the law.

Whether we are concerned that guns can be abused as weapons of violence or that our right to protect ourselves and our families is in jeopardy, both views demonstrate care about the value of human life.

Gun control is an emotional issue for many. Some focus on their right to protect their home and family. Others mourn tragic family losses when firearms have been easily available and abused. Both concerns are legitimate. So once again we are faced with the question in these areas: What is the best way to balance competing concerns for the common good? This difficult topic demands a civil and respectful conversation to find a way through.

THE WEST and the rising rest are poised to compete over principles, status, and geopolitical interests as the global turn proceeds. The challenge for the West and the rest alike is to forge a new and pluralistic order—one that preserves stability and a rules-based international system amid the multiple versions of modernity that will populate the next world.

—CHARLES A. KUPCHAN, *NO ONE'S WORLD: THE WEST, THE RISING REST, AND THE COMING GLOBAL TURN*

WE HAVE defined developing countries so as to encompass five billion of the six billion people in the world. But not all developing countries are the same. Those where development has failed face intractable problems not found in countries that are succeeding. We have, in fact, done the easier part of global development; finishing the job will be more difficult. Finish it we must, because an impoverished ghetto of one billion people will be increasingly impossible for a comfortable world to tolerate. . . .

To build a unity of purpose, thinking needs to change, not just within developmental agencies but among wider electorates whose views shape what is possible. Without an informed electorate, politicians will continue to use the bottom billion merely for photo opportunities, rather than promoting real transformation.

—PAUL COLLIER, *THE BOTTOM BILLION: WHY THE POOREST COUNTRIES ARE FAILING AND WHAT CAN BE DONE ABOUT IT*

8

Foreign Policy and Globalization

National Interest or Common Good?

THE ISSUES of globalization and foreign policy are too big and complex for one chapter. The quotation below introduces a real, three-dimensional tension that faces the human condition and foreign policy. Dani Rodrik, in *The Globalization Paradox*, says the following:

> We cannot simultaneously pursue democracy, national determination, and economic globalization. If you want to push globalization further, we have to give up either the nation state or democratic politics. If we want to maintain and deepen democracy, we have to choose between the nation state and international economic integration. And if we want to keep the nation state and self determination, we have to choose between deepening democracy and deepening globalization. Our troubles have their roots in our reluctance to face up to these ineluctable choices.[1]

In these few pages, we cannot cover the various ways and diverse issues that are embedded in the modern array of foreign policy choices. All we can do is discuss in a basic way the moral vision that religious values contribute to this area. The point of this chapter is not to form specific policy but to consider what needs to be included in thinking about global issues.

Foreign policy is a mix of:

- multinational politics
- competing military power
- global and national economics
- multiple internal national concerns
- issues of poverty, property, and national resources

All of these features have become more complicated with (1) the rise of globalization and (2) the increased multinational networking involved in both geopolitics and global economics.

So, as Rodrik's above comment suggests, foreign policy and globalization present us with some difficult choices: either we must make national choices at the expense of the globe or work toward globalization at the expense of national interest—all the while making sure that core human needs are increasingly met for those who have no power at all.

Either we must make national choices at the expense of the globe or work toward globalization at the expense of national interest—all the while making sure that core human needs on the globe are increasingly met.

Simply put, it is a daunting task, made more complex by the myriad of distinct and competing self-interests at every turn of the discussion. All we can hope to do in a single chapter is wrestle with principles in dealing with the tension between seeking national interests and being a good global partner.

BIBLICAL VALUES THAT SPEAK TO THE CHALLENGE

Issues of human care and globalization fall under the most basic mandates of Scripture—values that Jesus also affirmed. In Genesis 1, the creation of man and woman in God's image led to the call to manage the creation by exercising *dominion* over it—which involves the proper use and distribution of resources—and *subduing* it by controlling it well.

The judgment, reasoning, and assessment skills that humans possess distinguish us from other living beings in the creation—birds, fish, and animals. These attributes, along with creativity, are part of what makes up the image of God in us. So how we govern, share resources, and get along reflects whether or not we are living out the capabilities God gave to us regarding how to manage the earth.

Here are some things that Jesus and other biblical writers said that bring light to the topic at hand:

- Mark 12:28–31: Jesus said the whole Law can be summarized in two commands: "*'Love the Lord your God with all your heart, with all your soul, with all your mind, and with all your strength.' The second is: 'Love your neighbor as yourself.' There is no other commandment greater than these.*"

- Matthew 25:31–46: How we care for one another is so important that Jesus built a parable and the picture of judgment around it. In this parable from Matthew, the people of the nations are separated into sheep and goats, with the sheep being saved and the goats judged. Jesus says to the sheep: *"Come, you who are blessed by my Father. . . . For I was hungry and you gave me food, I was thirsty and you gave me something to drink, I was a stranger and you invited me in, I was naked and you gave me clothing, I was sick and you took care of me, I was in prison and you visited me."* In this passage, Jesus is calling his listeners to care for other followers of Jesus: *"Just as you did it for one of the least of these brothers or sisters of mine, you did it for me."*
- Luke 10:25–27: In the parable of the Good Samaritan, the call to care for others extends to anyone—even those we might not regard as a neighbor. In other words, in terms of basic human care and caring, there should be no nationalism or sectarianism that casts a blind eye toward others.
- Galatians 6:10: In this passage, Paul says it well: *"Let us do good to all people, especially to those who belong to the family of the faith."* All people deserve access to the well-being God's creation can provide when we use those resources wisely and well.
- Revelation 18: This passage portrays a different insight. It condemns and judges a world system that is solely built on greed and taking advantage of others. It rebukes the strong who take advantage of the weak and proclaims judgment upon those who take advantage of others.
- Micah 6:8: Rather than a world system built on greed and taking advantage, Scripture calls for compassion and sensitivity in how the world's affairs are managed. It warns against a selfishness that falls into oppression. *"He has told*

*you, O man, what is good, and what the LORD really wants
from you: He wants you to promote justice, to be faithful,
and to live obediently before your God."*

- Revelation 18 from yet another angle: This passage raises
  another issue for some readings of that book. The picture
  of a one-world government that throws the world into
  total chaos has led many to shy away from any multinational institutions and efforts out of fear that these efforts
  will lead into the very scenario that Revelation might be
  describing. Thus, many are skeptical of organizations, like
  the United Nations, NATO, and the EU, where rules are
  set for what all nations are to do.

  However, this concern fails to note an important distinction in what many such organizations are. What they
  often seek to promote is a mutual cooperation between
  nations rather than direct sovereignty over them. These
  organizations function for the world much like a neighborhood association works for families in a residential
  location. As long as national sovereignty is honored as
  nations participate in such organizations, then such concerns do not apply.

APPLYING BIBLICAL VALUES
IN A COMPLEX WORLD

Part of what makes foreign policy so difficult to discuss are the
various levels at which it works. There are elements of it that are
tied to the economy and in which governments do not always
have a direct involvement. National interests and economic
concerns often play against each other and produce a key factor
in what governments choose to do.

We have seen this reality at work in the recent events in Ukraine. Here we have a case where one country's sovereignty was violated by another when Russia took control of the Crimea. Russia's justification for the intervention was that they had to step in to protect Russian citizens—at the request of those citizens—and that Russia's previous history of possessing the Crimea gave her the right to intervene.

There are elements of foreign policy that are tied to the economy and in which governments do not always have a direct involvement.

It did not matter to Russia that such an act actually violated a treaty agreement Russia had signed with Ukraine, guaranteeing Ukraine's integrity and safety after Ukraine honored a request to give up her nuclear stockpile to lessen tensions in the area. A gracious act by Ukraine had left her exposed. A moral trust was violated.

This seeming breach of international law went practically uncontested because Russia possesses a veto at the United Nations and because the countries that protested did not want to intervene militarily, as this was seen as unrealistic and undesirable.

The lesson in this example is that the relationship between nations requires some level of mutual respect for issues of sovereignty or else relationships between nations will become more perilous than they already are. In the issue of Ukraine, efforts by those who rejected Russia's explanation moved in an economic direction. To make a moral statement and exact punishment, many nations proposed a series of sanctions. To preserve some sense of moral order for the future, the view was that something had to be done—especially given the fact that the claimed unjust abuse of Russian citizens in Ukraine was an issue the Ukrainians had said they would correct.

But a funny thing happened on the way to issuing sanctions that would show the displeasure of Russia's neighbors and act as the world's statement about an action most nations recognized as wrong. The idea of sanctions met with a completely different response in Europe than it did in the United States—a response that could undercut their effectiveness. The reason for the different reactions was the depth of business Europe had with Russia. European businesses were far more likely to feel the impact of European sanctions than American companies would from American sanctions. The cost of making a moral statement was undercut by the economic cost that would come with that statement.

All of this indicates the real and tenuous nature of international relationships when trying to uphold a moral stance in the world when so many interests and self-interests are in play.

Ukraine is but one example. We could point to events in Syria and in large parts of Africa where concerns about sovereignty—as well as the complexities of competing geopolitical and/or religious interests—allow these circumstances to fester. By all normal accounts, these situations are also seen as unjust and inhumane, since Syria has chosen to use outlawed chemical weapons, while murder and kidnapping are common in many of the struggles in Africa. The situation is even more complicated in some of these countries where human atrocities are taking place.

Add to this mix hybrid movements like ISIS that thrive in some countries where weak sovereignty exists. ISIS and Al

Qaeda operate outside national structures and hide behind the sovereignty claims of the many nations in which they exist. They also take advantage of the fact that many nations refuse to cooperate in order to protect their own individual security and economic interests. How do we fight a movement that does not have a visible public government and has opted out of operating with any moral constraint?

All of this makes for an uphill battle when applying the values of justice and compassion in practical ways—there are just too many distinct interests in play. The only way to limit everyone from doing what is right in his or her own eyes is to foster a level of international cooperation that could be effective if it could be exercised.

Some Americans look at the complexities and expense of these involvements and argue that the United States should be much less involved in world affairs. So some say, "Let the world tumble into its chaos. Mind the home front."

So some say, "Let the world tumble into its chaos.
Mind the home front."

However, the very economic factors we just described mean that many of our own national interests are tied up in what takes place globally. Withdrawing is not a real option. The decisions we face nationally are about choosing between extending our involvements and using our influence versus exercising restraint for reasons usually tied to the feasibility of success and/or to the level of the expense.

Three principles guide our discussion here, since getting into a detailed approach to this wide area is not possible:

- First, the nature of globalization and the central role of the United States in the world order and commerce mean we cannot be disengaged from the world scene. Everything is too intertwined for us to withdraw. We have to be globally aware and involved.
- Second, as people created in God's image, we have a moral responsibility to seek justice. That is part of being a good global neighbor and partner.
- Third, we do this with an awareness that we are but one citizen in a global village. We have to respect the rights of other nations just as we seek to have our rights as a nation be respected.

It is perhaps fortunate that our political parties are usually slow to play too much politics with most issues that are tied to foreign affairs. Accountability takes place at the ballot box. Unlike issues in domestic policy, the executive branch has a fairly free hand in how foreign policy is executed, although this latitude has begun to shrink in recent decades no matter who is in power. In order to be a dexterous player in a dangerous world, our framing of these complex issues must be broad enough to appreciate all the factors at work and flexible enough to react quickly in a world where things happen faster and with more global awareness than ever before. We also need to be open enough to appreciate that complexity as we search for solutions to the difficult choices we often face.

Once again we can see legitimate concerns on both sides of the debate ledger. It means that sometimes we will choose to get involved and other times we will step back. There is no one-size-fits-all principle here. The situations are too complex and too diverse to determine solutions through a single lens. Thinking in sound bites or buzzwords is not enough.

These realities make selective alliance building and wise co-operative engagement imperative when and where they can be developed. If nations do not hold one another accountable in some ways for their actions, it is more likely that there will be a powerful and disruptive rogue state or states. If hybrid entities can function with impunity as recently took place with the mass slayings in Paris, then the world becomes a very danger-ous, even hostile place. The world and its interlaced relation-ships become more unstable. If governments and businesses do not figure out how to cooperate with one another economically versus competing with one another, not only will resources be poorly distributed and competition rule the day with escalating self-interests, but the opportunity to be more efficiently and ef-fectively humane will disappear. Without some form of global cooperation, hybrids cannot be dealt with decisively. There is no way to opt out of being in the world.

AGAIN, ARE WE ASKING THE RIGHT QUESTIONS?

Given the importance of economics alongside the political di-mension, how we use, abuse, and distribute resources becomes an important, even key, question—both morally and practically— for how nations relate to one another. In some ways, businesses are a kind of government. Businesses operate like independent nations in certain key sectors of our international society. They also possess competing concerns. They rule and manage impor-tant spheres of human affairs. This is why we see things like the G8 and G20 talks. Getting these various spheres to coordinate with one another is important when it can be done.

Part of the moral burden for how we engage in the world and care for those most needy lies with those who control and benefit from the distribution of the resources humans produce. How badly the world needs a sense of compassion can be seen by how exposed many of the poor are—not only to life lived on the edge of survival but to exposure to all sorts of violence.[2] Jesus was known for caring about the marginalized, but much of the world turns a blind eye to such needs. Some of our neighbors are quite invisible. Our global world requires global cooperation at some level, and that cooperation extends far beyond what governments do and can do.

Jesus was known for caring about the marginalized, but much of the world turns a blind eye to such needs.

Removing national or business interests from the foreign policy equation is not possible. So as we pursue foreign policy, we must be realistic about all the factors in play. Posing questions about foreign policy merely in terms of national government interest versus international cooperation places the discussion on too limited a playing field. Seeing foreign policy only in this light fails to get at the issues humanity or any particular nation faces. The depth of such problems requires concern and cooperation from both government and business—and in some cases coordination.

The ability of nonprofit and religious organizations to step in also adds a final dimension to the possibilities. Nonprofit and religious relief and presence have often been the best link to helping people trapped in the more difficult locations of our world. Here is one sphere where the presence of religiously motivated compassion has been a positive story. It needs to be appreciated and promoted.

So ... What Would Jesus Say about National Interest versus International Common Good?

This topic is a particularly difficult one to apply biblical principles to, but there are some key principles that *do* apply:

- Throughout Jesus' ministry on earth, he was known for caring about the marginalized.
- Jesus taught that when we treat others with compassion and care, we are doing the same for him.
- As people created in God's image, we have a moral responsibility to seek justice.
- The call to care for others extends to everyone—even those we may not consider neighbors.
- We are called to promote justice and live obediently before God in how the world's affairs are managed.

If we choose to follow the teachings of Jesus and the Bible, we have some very concrete principles to apply to a very complex issue. As on all the issues discussed in this book, meaningful, open conversation is needed if we are to make any headway in improving our relationship to the rest of the world—a world that God has given to us to steward and manage well.

MILITARY RESOURCES can implement four types of actions that are the modalities or currencies of military power. Military resources can be used to (1) physically fight and destroy; (2) back up threats in coercive diplomacy; (3) promise protection, including peacekeeping; and (4) provide many forms of assistance.

—JOSEPH S. NYE, JR., *THE FUTURE OF POWER*

9

War and Peace

"Just War" or Pacifism?

THE ROLE of the military and the function of war has changed in many ways since World War II. The presence of nuclear arsenals and the rise of undeclared wars that do not involve countries but rather individual hybrid groups with access to technology and weapons have changed how military might is used. They have raised new questions about the policies necessary to maintain peace in the world. The topic of war and peace is a broad one and could take many directions, but certain issues are fundamental to any discussion on this topic.

So this chapter considers two public issues tied to the military: (1) moral rights in terms of war, and (2) the use of power in a world where because of the rise of terrorism, battles are not just between countries, and national governments are not directly involved.

These changes and new realities mean that how we view the

role of the military and the moral use of power needs careful reflection.

Placing This Topic in Its Larger Political and Economic Context

Defending a people is not cheap. Defense spending has hovered mostly between 20 and 25 percent of our federal spending from 2011 into projections for 2016. We spend by far more money on our military than any other country. After us come China, Russia, Saudi Arabia, and France.[1] We spent $618.7 billion on defense while China spent $171.4 billion and Russia expended $84.9 billion. Only health care (between 23 and 28 percent) and pensions tied to Social Security (between 21 and 23 percent) account for as much of the budget as our military does, depending on which year we are considering. These three areas are the bulk of our federal spending, comprising together about three-fourths of the total expense.[2] Our expense for welfare, for example, is less than half of any of these three categories (at 9 to 13 percent). By comparison, education sits at 3 percent.

How We Are Spending Our Money

Clearly when it comes to our politics, the budgetary numbers tell us that our key issues are defense, health care, and a variety of social programs (entitlements like Social Security and Medicare, welfare, plus education). These three areas easily consume the largest part of our public expenditure at around 85 percent of the total budget. The expenses in these areas show that we are a generous nation, regardless of our specific political views, pooling many resources in taxes and social program pay-ins to help one another.

The expenses in these areas show that
we are a generous nation, regardless
of our specific political views.

Can We Afford to Be Generous?

But there is only so much room in terms of what we can afford to do. Balancing these large areas of spending—including spending on defense—is actually one of the biggest political problems we face, because of the pressure it places on raising taxes and being fiscally responsible. When we debate with one another about how high our taxes are or should be, we are actually discussing a series of areas that compete within a demanding set of corporate budgetary commitments and responsibilities. This is especially the case when the pool of younger people paying into the system is not as large as the growing number of older people who are coming to draw on these entitlements. Add to this the inherent tension between earning a living as an individual (and the right we have to the resources we earn) versus the need to reflect on how generous we want to be and how much generosity we can afford, and you have the key formula for what creates legislative gridlock, as people land on different sides of the divide about how to cut up this complex pie and pay for it. And a big part of this pie has to do with war and peace.

Negotiations Need to Consider All Issues

When we pursue budgetary policy but take areas like health care, pensions, elements of welfare, and defense off the table, we limit room for serious maneuver in assessing our priorities, not to mention getting control of a large deficit. When we look at only one side of the equation—whether it be raising funds through taxes or limiting them—we also make it next to impossible to make progress. As with most of the other issues discussed in this book, we need to find a way through by negotiating with both sides of the equation as part of the discussion, versus digging in on our views even before we head into conversation. When we take certain programs completely off the discussion table, we limit our options— especially when those programs represent such a large portion of our budget.

Rather than jumping to shut the government down when we get stuck, we need to wrestle with what is an appropriate level of expenditure on defense (as well as other large areas) versus how much sacrifice we should make for others.

Authentic discussion is needed to balance these competing tensions with an awareness that we all are legitimately contending for areas and concerns where multiple judgments are in play.

BIBLICAL TEACHINGS ON THE
ISSUES OF PACIFISM AND WAR

Some of the same biblical principles that we looked at in our discussion of gun control apply here as well. A strong and venerable part of Christianity argues for pacifism mainly on the basis of Jesus' teaching at the Sermon on the Mount, where the idea of retaliation and violence is repudiated at a personal level (Matthew 5:38–42; Luke 6:27–30).[3]

- Matthew 5:38-39a: *"You have heard that it was said, 'An eye for an eye and a tooth for a tooth.' But I say to you, do not resist the evildoer."*
- Matthew 5:9: Beyond this Jesus teaches *"Blessed are the peacemakers, for they will be called the children of God."*
- Matthew 26:52: When Jesus' opponents came to arrest him and Peter reacted by cutting off a servant's ear, *"Jesus said to [Peter], 'Put your sword back in its place! For all who take hold of the sword will die by the sword.'"*

Adding together these teachings, you build a case that many accept as a call for pacifism among Christians.[4] Anabaptists and Mennonites are among the groups that accept some form of pacifism as reflective of Jesus' teaching.[5]

- Luke 3:14: The New Testament does not blatantly reject all violence or use of coercive power. John the Baptist recognized the role of a soldier in bringing social order. We see this in how John responded to some soldiers who asked him an important question about what repentance looked like for them. *"Then some soldiers also asked him, 'And as for us—what should we do?' He told them, 'Take money from no one by violence or by false accusation, and be content with your pay.'"* John the Baptist does not tell the soldiers to quit their jobs, but to exercise their use of governmental power responsibly and justly.
- Romans 13:1–7: Paul speaks of governments having the right to bear the sword, which means they have the right

to use coercive force, watch over their citizens, and collect taxes.

- The Book of Revelation shows God in battle and discusses a worldwide war that Jesus, in part, wages for justice and for judgment that punishes evil. Revelation 19:11–21 portrays this quite vividly.
- The Old Testament portrays God as using nations to punish other nations, showing us yet another example of moral tension in Scripture, which calls for discernment.
- The Prophets: The prophets, like Isaiah, give evidence of this kind of engagement between nations. Isaiah 45 describes this role for a non-Israelite king, Cyrus. National accountability is a way justice takes place and global order is maintained. We are to pursue and seek peace as much as is possible, but nations have the right, and even obligation, to self-defense.

"JUST WAR"

This tension has resulted in the development of a morally reflective tradition, known as "just war" theory, better called *justified war*. Regarding justified war, the question is, When is the use of violence morally defensible?[6] When is it proper to go to war?

The tradition of justified war has roots in the writing of Augustine (345–430), but actually is older, as even Augustine's mentor—Ambrose (340–369)—taught these ideas, and other discussion and debate on the matter are present in patristic writings of the first few centuries of Christianity.[7]

A justified war view is really a position between seeking war as a raw use of power[8] and pacifism. Justified war is skeptical about the raw use of power and its potential for abuse. It recognizes the need for judgment and discernment in a dysfunctional, fallen world and points to respect and accountability for nations among the peoples of the world. And it accepts that self-defense and intervention are appropriate forms of response to unjust aggression and oppression.[9] Just war is used to protect the innocent, recover what has been wrongly taken, defend against a wrongful attack, and punish evil.

Just war is used to protect the innocent, recover what has been wrongly taken, defend against a wrongful attack, and punish evil.

Justifying war applies many standards to determine when the use of force in response to a challenge is justified. The very listing of these features shows the discernment called for in the use of power, given the awareness that with war comes hard choices—many of them not for good, but questions of a lesser evil.

So, for example, a lesser evil argument is how Dietrich Bonhoeffer described his dilemma in opting to participate in Hitler's assassination so as to stop a devastating world war. Here are the factors that lead to a defense of the use of lethal force:[10]

1. War must have a just cause, being fundamentally a defensive war.
2. It must have a just intention, to secure a fair peace for all parties. This excludes national revenge, economic exploitation, and ethnic cleansing.
3. It must be a last resort. All diplomatic efforts should be pursued and continued.

4. Properly constituted authorities must declare it. War is the work of states.

5. It must have limited objectives and no annihilation of the enemy.

6. It must use proportionate means, sufficient to deter the aggression. The use of nuclear weapons becomes a real point of debate here. Generally such weapons are not seen as moral because they are indiscriminate in their killing. They exist as deterrents against others who possess such weapons.

7. It must respect noncombatant immunity, including wounded soldiers or prisoners of war. Weapons of indiscriminate mass destruction are immoral.

8. The more international recognition and support there is the better.

Debated in "just war" theory is whether a preemptive strike is ever justified. Those who support such a strike argue that an imminent self-defense is allowed.

This position is rooted in biblical and Christian values and argues that nations should defend their people and have access to military power with restricted goals. These restrictions are tied to genuine self-protection and the maintenance of some level of accountability among nations.

THE COMPLICATING FACTOR OF A NEW KIND OF WAR

What has made this discussion more complicated in recent times is the presence of what has been called "hybrid war." The question here is not about a battle of nation against nation, nor does it involve formal declarations of war. Here the opponent—usually some form of terrorism—involves non-government entities that use weapons and means of power previously tied to nation-states. This kind of unseen enemy plays by no rules other than opportunity, and their form of engagement complicates the application of justified war standards. Even so, the commitment of a nation's right to self-defense and protection of the innocent applies.

This hybrid form of war, along with the development of technology, has raised another new element to war: the use of drones and the issue of national sovereignty. If and when a nation harbors or cannot cope with the presence of a non-national terror group, what rules of sovereignty apply? How does—and even can—the older approach of "just war" help to guide decisions about this new hybrid war? We need freshly formed questions and answers because we're dealing with a new kind of war.

If and when a nation harbors or cannot cope with the presence of a non-national terror group, what rules of sovereignty apply?

This hybrid war is a detail in the war-peace conversation that needs more discussion at a moral level. We note it here in passing as a topic all its own that requires more space than we have here. To the extent that governments have the right to protect their people from attack and that these terrorist organizations are not nations but "floating" entities hiding under the protection that being in a foreign nation can give either willingly or unwillingly, it is a topic that can and should be broached.

One thing seems clear after the array of attacks on people

in public places and planes in 2015: the hybrid, multinational nature of the use of violence requires multinational cooperation on a scale rarely required previously. To be effective, policy will challenge any nation's sense of *national* security, because this is a case of *international* security—since we are dealing with a movement that often takes advantage of internal governmental weakness and seeks to demolish the national entities in which it operates.

When weak nations are attacked from within, how should their ineffective sovereignty be seen when other nations are placed at risk? In other words, how do we fight a war with a non-nation that is operating with impunity within a nation too weak to oppose it? None of the answers are easy, nor are they inexpensive, because of what is required to track the threat. Without concentrated and widespread cooperation on many fronts, there is little chance of success.

THE ISSUE OF NUCLEAR PROLIFERATION

Another controversial aspect of this topic is the prospect of nuclear proliferation. Controlling the spread of nuclear weapons is a goal that matches the quest for global peace: the fewer weapons of mass destruction, the less chance they will fall into the wrong hands for the wrong use. But controlling nuclear proliferation has also become more complicated—especially among nations that have declared that they wish to see their avowed enemies eliminated.

Add into this mix the fact that some of these same countries have even more radical forces in their midst who have shown they will not hesitate to act violently against their enemies, and the situation looks even more precarious. Of course, recent discussion of the treaty with Iran, alongside the prospect of ISIS, is in view here, especially given both Iran and ISIS's publically declared goal to eliminate Israel.

The dilemma is whether it's possible to craft a genuine and effective treaty with someone whose goals include eliminating another legitimately recognized nation—even if they claim to provide verification and access to their nuclear facilities. On the one hand, limiting nuclear weapons is clearly a benefit to all, but whether we can trust the signees is central to an agreement's viability. Perhaps the oddest irony in this case is that this is one of the few areas where Obama administration policy and Russian policy have aligned in pursuing an agreement.

You might think that an agreement that limits nuclear weapons in a particular state would require that nation's recognition of other states' right to exist. We do not have that kind of Iranian commitment to Israel here. Without this recognition, such an agreement should be viewed with a degree of skepticism about whether the state can accomplish what it sets out to do—even when the affirmed goal is worthy. Any such agreement should be carefully scrutinized, lest it become only an empty piece of paper.

Biblical values do not permit people made in God's image to eliminate others just because they are different. The Holocaust was a real lesson regarding what people who hate are capable of doing. Recent violent events in Egypt and France show that people are still capable of vile acts.

Defending a value that protects nations and life needs to remain a priority. But thinking only about nuclear proliferation may not be enough to get us to the ultimate goal of making the world safe for its people.

OTHER USES OF POWER

The issue of war and peace is not the only role for a military presence. Nations use soldiers for other kinds of community work and presence. It is here that the quotation that opened our chapter falls, for it describes four roles in the geopolitical use of power that extend beyond war: (1) to physically fight and destroy; (2) to back up threats; (3) to grant protection, including peacekeeping; and (4) to provide forms of assistance.

When we think about foreign policy and the use of the military, these other dimensions of military presence are important. Military force not only defends freedom, it makes a case for what freedom represents and holds others accountable with its potential threatening power. The mere prospect of power can back up threats in coercive diplomacy.

Whether we think about nuclear capability or sheer military power, we need only think about what NATO has meant to the security of Europe to see that this kind of military presence can yield a more peaceful result than might have existed otherwise. As odd as it sounds, military power can actually yield peacekeeping, because the alternative of one-sided military might unchecked is far less attractive.

Finally, the military can provide logistics, which allow for disaster relief and other forms of assistance. This kind of service brings a sense of appreciation from those who experience it. I recall a conversation I once had with a German as we observed the fiftieth anniversary of World War II while I was on a sabbatical of study in Germany. He told me he has always appreciated the United States because the GIs distributed food to him when he was a young child at the end of the war.

The role of the American military is an important dimension of our foreign policy and can be a deterrent force in the world. Because we are a major world power, it is a responsibility we shoulder. The crucial part the military plays in our role in the world is, perhaps, the one topic that politicians in Washington agree on. The ongoing debates focus on which particular involvements are wise and how deeply we should or should not go when we use our troops—often in ways that do not reflect all-out war.

The ongoing debates focus on which particular involvements are wise and how deeply we should or should not go when we use our troops.

Most current involvement is either in hybrid wars, efforts to limit violence in other parts of the world, or by showing military presence to keep the peace. These are clearly case-by-case decisions. A key is that once the course to act is taken, care still needs to be exercised to ensure that combatants are the ones who are engaged and that abuses of the exercise of power are avoided.

We also need to be sure the goals we set are achievable and worth the expense and risk of our soldiers' lives. We should not start what cannot be finished. Given that presence can be deterrence, we also need to be sure that if we withdraw, the result is not a return to the chaos we originally tried to stop. It is a counterproductive use of troops to have an effort reversed and sacrifices rendered void because we would not stay the course and see the goal through.

POINTS OF AGREEMENT

The sheer importance of our military's role in the world is an exception to the rule of governmental gridlock. Political parties in Washington work harder toward a cohesive and united approach—sometimes debating and sometimes compromising. Everyone senses that the common good can only be maintained when the country is secure and when the peace is diligently kept through a powerful presence. Everyone bites the bullet of economic sacrifice to achieve these results. Everyone also wants to communicate appreciation to those who serve the country and place their lives in harm's way. So we often are quick to be sure our military personnel have all they need to do their jobs. When these standards are violated, as was the case with the recent issue over poor medical care of veterans, there is a national reaction that does work across party lines.

Our glimpse of the military reveals that how we use our army, navy, air force, and marines is not always a matter of whether or not to go to war. There are many intermediate levels of engagement with other nations that actually work to keep the peace. Political discussions we have here involve tensions in which the controlled use of violence is designed to prevent more violence. The goal is to make sure peace is maintained with someone who otherwise might take advantage of a vacuum of power. Perhaps a key lesson from this discussion is that we can move forward in any area if we collectively do a better job of putting our minds to it and work harder together to work things out. On this topic the common good seems to be more instinctive and mostly works.

So . . . What Would Jesus Say about War and Peace?

Once again, this complicated issue is spoken to in the teachings of Jesus and the pages of the Bible. Though personal retribution is discouraged and the call is to love one's enemy, national responsibility to protect is not voided by such moral concerns. Tough judgments again abound when particular cases are brought forward. Let's look at the biblical principles that can be applied to this issue:

- *"Do not resist the evildoer"* (Matthew 5:38). When Jesus came to earth, he strongly taught that he was overturning the Old Testament standard of an "eye for an eye." The new standard involved nonviolence.
- *"Peacemakers are blessed"* (Matthew 5:9).
- *"Non-retaliation was commanded when Jesus was being arrested"* (Matthew 26:52).
- *"Under certain circumstances, we are to take up the sword."* Jesus told his disciples as they went out to teach others: *"But now . . . the one who has no sword must sell his cloak and buy one"* (Luke 22:36). Here we see the balance in Jesus' teaching: sometimes, acting in self-defense is permitted.
- *"The government has the right to use force to punish evil doers"* (Romans 13:1–7).
- *"In Old Testament times, God sometimes used one nation to punish another."*

The to-and-fro of genuine debate and reflection with mutual respect is what we need. In this area, we tend more often than not to get there. The expenses in this area show that we are a generous nation, regardless of our specific political views, pooling many resources in taxes and social program pay-ins to try to help each other and reaching out in a dangerous world to try and make it a safer place. If that kind of give and take can work here, why not in other areas?

"CAN WE, can we get along?"

—RODNEY KING IN AN INTERVIEW
DURING 1992 L.A. RIOTS

Race

Equality, Violence, and Justice

RACE HAS always been a contentious issue in the United
States. Starting with slavery and moving through the Civil War,
no topic has produced more domestic violence and disagreement within the country than this one. The initial divide became regional when the South—in an attempt to defend states'
rights and the region's economic and social system—seceded
from the Union to defend the right to own slaves. The battle
lasted from 1861 to 1865. Abraham Lincoln became a national
hero for his effort in keeping the Union together. Today that
battle's shadow is still being fought in many ways—including
controversies tied to flying the Confederate flag and the use of
its symbol in some states, as well as the use of police force in
some situations.

In between, we have had the Civil Rights Movement, with
Martin Luther King, Jr., becoming another national hero as he
led the nonviolent protests and gave the now famous "I Have

a Dream" speech on the Washington mall on August 28, 1963. Most major civil rights legislation was passed in 1964. In 1868, the thirteenth amendment—a Reconstruction amendment— outlawed slavery and discrimination on the basis of race by giving an entire race the full citizenship they had been previously denied. But it took almost one hundred years for the legislative cycle to catch up to the values of what that amendment sought to achieve.

Despite all of this legislative and national history, even now and again things explode. In August 1965, Los Angeles went through the violent and shocking Watts riots. In 1992, riots again broke out, in reaction to a verdict finding innocent the officers who pursued Rodney King in a high-speed car chase and then subdued and beat him upon capture. A federal case a year later did convict two of the four officers. An early use of video from a private citizen showing the brutality of the beating sparked a national reaction and debate.

More recently a series of incidents has again brought race to the fore. In August 2014, Ferguson, Missouri, saw riots in reaction to the shooting of an African-American suspected of stealing and fleeing the scene. In April 2015, Baltimore also exploded when an African-American was beaten and eventually died from injuries sustained while being restrained by police. These are but some of the most famous of incidents to date. Other incidents involve African-American women, such as the teenaged girl subdued by a McKinney, Texas, officer who later resigned when the video of his actions went viral; and Sandra Bland, who committed suicide in Texas after being violently subdued for failing to use a turn signal and then refusing to respond to an officer's instructions when he pulled her over. A *New York Times/ CBS News* poll taken in the aftermath of all of this has nearly six in ten Americans saying race relations are bad, with four in ten saying they are getting worse.[1] This is in stunning contrast to 2008–2009, when two-thirds said those relations were generally good. It takes more than legislation to get along.

THE CURRENT BATTLE LINES

On one side of the spectrum, some believe that many of these situations escalated because police—in their pursuit of lawbreakers—were uncertain about whether or not a gun had been drawn. There are also complaints about disrespectful attitudes from people who are stopped. Others think that the cause is the use of excessive force, which underscores continuing racism and injustice among some in the society—including some police. Another complaint comes from people who are stopped in certain neighborhoods for no other reason than suspicion because of their race.

These incidents are symptomatic of a core distrust that exists, especially between blacks and whites, in large parts of our society. Each side can point to elements in these events showing that the other side was wrong. A sense of injustice coming from each side fuels the gridlock of the push-pull reactions and counterreactions. Now and again the spiral explodes.

These incidents are symptomatic of a core distrust that exists, especially between blacks and whites, in large parts of our society.

What is interesting about this issue is that it does not really line up in the common conservative-liberal standoff when it comes to the goal. There is a consensus that race relations need to improve and that good race relations are desirable. A substantial majority of people of all races want to go there.

But it is hard for a racial majority to appreciate what being a racial minority with our unique racial history can mean for those on the other end. Even in a country where so much protective legislation exists and has been passed as the law of the land, many African-Americans feel a deep sense of injustice. I once asked an African-American pastor and friend, Tony Evans, what Caucasians did not understand about living as a black in America. His answer was vivid and powerful as he shared a series of experiences where he was pulled over in a more-white-than-black neighborhood—not because he had done anything wrong, but simply because he was black. The question was always, "What are you doing here?"[2]

THE BIBLICAL DISCUSSION

Reconciliation is a core biblical value. Beyond the core call to love one's neighbor as oneself, part of what Jesus called the Great Commandment (Mark 12:31), there are significant texts that point to reconciliation between people (usually seen as Jews and Gentiles) whose previous history was one of distrust, violence, and religious difference. We'll mention four specific passages here.

Ephesians 2:11–22: Verses 14–19 say, *"For [Jesus] is our peace, the one who made both groups into one and who destroyed the middle wall of partition, the hostility. . . . He did this to create in himself one new man out of two, thus making peace, and to reconcile them both in one body to God through the cross, by which the hostility has been killed. . . . So then you are no longer foreigners and noncitizens, but you are fellow citizens with the saints and members of God's household."* This passage beautifully shows that one of Jesus' goals is to draw people together. Here Paul is talking specifically about Jews and Gentiles—another situation where hatred and hostility shaped interaction—but that is also very applicable to our current racial hostility in the United States. Paul was writing to two groups who shared a mutual appreciation for what God had done for them, encouraging them to better appreciate each other. Since all people are made in God's image and we are together called to be good stewards of our creation, Paul calls us all to work together for God's purposes. The work of Jesus on the cross shows the value of forgiveness in the face of wrongs committed, also calling these once-enemy groups to forgive each other. Sharing in his forgiveness gives a basis for unity that is to transcend race.

Luke 3:14: There is another, less well-known text that also is at work in this discussion. In Luke 3:14, soldiers ask John the Baptist what they should do in regard to repentance. John replies, *"Do not extort money from anyone by threats or by false accusation, and be content with your wages."* (ESV) The application to race relations is that being in a position of authority does not give a person the right to abuse the use of that authority. So John's exhortation contains a call to be careful with how power is used, even in the context of law enforcement. The response by authorities to be avoided in John's command is surely one that involves the use of power to extort desired funds.

Romans 13:1-2: On the other side, we must consider the responsibility people have to obey the law and not resort to violence. We've looked at this passage before, but its message is pertinent to this topic as well: *"Let every person be subject to the governing authorities. For there is no authority except by God's appointment, and the authorities that exist have been instituted by God. So the person who resists such authority resists the ordinance of God."*

One of the things that made Martin Luther King's protests so morally powerful was their nonviolent approach. The purpose of the protests was to expose the current laws and their injustice, in as nonviolent a way as possible. Respect for law was shown by a willingness to accept the penalty for any that was violated.

When Martin Luther King's marchers were beaten merely for protesting, the outcry that something was amiss became large and obvious. But when violence comes with protests that include looting and stealing, no sympathy for the cause of justice is generated and more distrust is built up. Injustice met with more injustice does not move people to reconcile. Anger mixed with lawbreaking does not engender a solution; it only raises the likelihood of a hard push-back.

Injustice met with more injustice
does not move people to reconcile.

---

1 John 4:20–21: The message here is a convicting one. As you read, consider how this applies to race relations: *"If anyone says, 'I love God,' and hates his brother, he is a liar; for he who does not love his brother whom he has seen cannot love God whom he has not seen. And this commandment we have from him: whoever loves God must also love his brother."* (ESV) While this passage speaks specifically to men and women who are brothers and sisters in Christ, the principle is broader, and the indictment is strong: if we say we love God yet hate our brother, we are *liars.* Jesus affirms this broader application when he defines the

two greatest commandments of all—the second one being to love our neighbors as ourselves (Mark 12:31). In this passage, "neighbor" is not restricted to fellow believers but applies to all of humanity.

WHY THE CHURCH MATTERS IN RACE

The gospel's emphasis on reconciliation means that churches can have a major role in helping people turn the corner on race. Pastors and churches are an important part of some of the most stable African-American communities.

Churches that are successful in bringing stability to this tense situation are traditionally involved in helping the community with local needs and with support to broken families. When riots broke out in Ferguson and in Baltimore, local pastors came together to join forces to calm the situation. Those relationships are still playing a significant part in keeping the peace in those regions.[3] This bridge-building effort involved both African-American pastors and those of other backgrounds.

This issue does not so much need fresh legislation as it needs a new approach and an understanding of what really brings change. The intentional grassroots involvement of community leaders certainly pushes things in a better direction and enters in at a place that legislation cannot reach.

MOVING BEYOND LEGISLATION

The history of racial relations between blacks and whites in America is not a pretty one. In this case, gridlock is not caused by legislative failure to create laws to address these issues. So this issue is distinct from most of the others we have traced. Legislation to deal with many of these issues already exists. There is a wide consensus that these laws are good and needed.

Rather, this is an issue of the heart and reflecting on how we actually treat and think about one another. All of us need to try to walk in one another's shoes. And we all need to learn from and apply the principles of community leadership that have been successful in keeping the peace and bridging the gap.

The legislation that is already in place can only work in a context of mutual understanding and hearts willing to forgive and reconcile. Only in such a context can new legislation surface and become appreciated as positive. Only when hearts are altered can systemic injustice be seen and reversed. To get along, we have to understand one another better in order to gain common good for all.

So . . . What Would Jesus Say about Race Relations?

In addition to the scriptures we looked at earlier in the chapter, several statements directly from Jesus (and one from Paul) leave little doubt as to what he would advise. One of Jesus' core messages—and the message of the entire Bible—is that of love. We cannot escape the essentiality of this simple but complex command, especially when love is difficult—either because of our own prejudices or because of the wrongs of others.

- *The second-greatest commandment.* For those of us who consider ourselves Christians, we must give utmost attention to Jesus' response to the upcoming question: "'Which commandment in the law is the greatest?' Jesus said to him,

'Love the Lord your God with all your heart, with all your soul, and with all your mind.' This is the first and greatest commandment. The second is like it: 'Love your neighbor as yourself.' All the law and the prophets depend on these two commandments" (Matthew 22:36–40).

- *Love those difficult to love.* Easy love is not worth much, as Jesus says in the upcoming passage. Loving under difficult circumstances is what pleases God. Here's what Jesus has to say: *"You have heard that it was said, 'Love your neighbor' and 'hate your enemy.' But I say to you, love your enemy and pray for those who persecute you. . . . For if you love those who love you, what reward do you have? . . . And if you only greet your brothers, what more do you do?"* (Matthew 5:43–47).

- *Jesus values peacemakers.* In Jesus' well-known beatitudes, he says, *"Blessed are the peacemakers, for they will be called the children of God"* (Matthew 5:9). In our country, there is much need for peacemaking—especially in the relationships between Americans of different colors.

- *Being angry with another is a serious thing.* In the Sermon on the Mount, a grouping of some of Jesus' core teachings, we read: *"You have heard that it was said to an older generation, 'Do not murder,' and 'whoever murders will be subjected to judgment.' But I say to you that anyone who is angry with a brother will be subjected to judgment"* (Matthew 5:21–22).

- *Jesus' parting command.* Of such importance is the command to love that Jesus spoke of loving others several times in his final words. Here he said, *"My commandment is this—to love one another just as I have loved you"* (John 15:12). Loving one another as Jesus loved us is the highest of callings. Even though Jesus knew this would not always be easy for us, he does not shrink back in his command that we do so. This text is about how disciples love each other, but the narrow principle is expanded when one considers the great commandment above.

- *Set things right; agree with one another.* Paul, at the close of his letter to the church at Corinth, summed up his words for this divided and contentious church. *"Finally, brothers and sisters, rejoice, set things right, be encouraged, agree with one another, live in peace, and the God of love and peace will be with you"* (2 Corinthians 13:11). What a beautiful message to a divided people—a message that is more than applicable to our situation today. Although this passage is addressed to a church community, it provides a path that should reflect all our relationships. Galatians 6:10 teaches, *"Let us do good to all people, especially to those who belong to the family of faith."*

As implied in all the above passages, loving others is often not an easy thing; but if we are to apply these biblical principles to the topic at hand, we must heed the powerful and difficult chief command of loving those who are made in the image of God—and that includes every one of us.

In this chapter, I have focused on relations between blacks and whites, but the issues apply to how any and all races and ethnicities should get along. As our country becomes more cross-cultural—with many more races and ethnicities more widely represented—the lessons of love urged here will require broad, multicultural application.

In the last several years, there has been a growing interest in pushing more students to go to college as one way to increase the skill level of our nation's workforce. As a part of this effort, new research has been conducted on what it means for students to be "college-ready." Achieve, a nonprofit educational organization created by the National Governors Association, recently interviewed three hundred instructors who taught first-year students in two- and four-year colleges. One of the most striking findings of the report is what these college teachers said students entering college were unprepared to do:

- 70 percent say students do not comprehend complex reading materials.
- 66 percent say students cannot think analytically.
- 65 percent say students lack appropriate work and study habits.
- 62 percent says students write poorly.
- 59 percent say students do not know how to do research.
- 55 percent say students can't apply what they have learned to solve problems.

11

Education

Relating to a Globalized World

DOES OUR current system of education educate?

This may seem a strange question, but the results of surveys like the one cited on the opposite page tell us that our efforts to educate are not yielding what we'd expected. Other statistics underscore the problem. Only 70 percent of American students graduate from high school. This rate lags behind countries like Denmark (96 percent), Japan (93 percent), Poland (92 percent), and Italy (79 percent).[1]

According to a study sponsored by the Bill & Melinda Gates Foundation, only a third of US high school graduates enroll in college, and only one in seven get a bachelor's degree. The number is worse for poor and minority students.[2] When 85 percent of current jobs and 90 percent of the best-paying future jobs require some secondary education, success in college is important for personal development. A college education *does* normally translate into a better quality of life in terms of jobs and income.[3] In 2002, the United States ranked tenth among industrial nations in the rate of college completion among twenty-five- to thirty-four-year-olds.[4] In 2010, the country ranked fourth in terms of overall college graduates.[5]

Our educational system is complex. Almost 100,000 schools are overseen by more than 14,000 school districts. The cost of public education, mostly a function of state and local revenues, is around $584 billion in a given year. More than 6 million people work in this sector, which is four times the size of our military.[6]

Education, like defense, is about our nation's well-being. We rarely think about education corporately. Our concern is usually much more personal—we care about our own children's and grandchildren's education. But the larger policy impacts us all, as our society functions in a competing world where the quality of our workforce significantly impacts our effectiveness. In discussing how we educate our collective mass of children, we may again be asking the wrong questions. Our children represent a different kind of world army—an army for productivity, creativity, and progress.

Education, like defense, is about our nation's well-being.

THE ORIGINS AND GOALS OF PUBLIC EDUCATION

Public education came after biblical times. The university was originally a product of monastic education, formally coming into existence in the eleventh century. Arts, and either theology, law, or medicine, dominated these early schools. Universities like Harvard and Yale were originally founded to form the character of their students and lead them to pursue their faith with a depth of knowledge. In the beginning, schooling children and university students was reserved for the more privileged classes. Public education is of recent vintage in the United States.

- *1852*: The first compulsory school law was passed in Massachusetts.
- *1918*: All children were compelled to attend schools by their states.
- *1954*: *Brown v. Board of Education* declared segregation illegal.

By comparison, schools in the UK date back as far as the Canterbury school, founded in 597. However, as in the United States, extensive public schooling did not arise until 1833–40, with compulsory education coming in 1880.

Public education for children today began as a societal goal of ensuring that all, especially the poor, received the core skills needed to engage with the Industrial Revolution.

Churches fueled the movement in Britain. In the United States, Horace Mann drove the public school movement as a way to civilize the masses. This statement from his twelfth annual report, given in 1848, shows his intent:

> *Education then, beyond all other devices of human origin, is a great equalizer of the conditions of men,—the balance wheel of the social machinery. I do not here mean that it so elevates the moral nature as to make men disdain and abhor the oppression of their fellow men. This idea pertains to another of its attributes. But I mean that it gives each man the independence and the means by which he can resist the selfishness of other men. It does better than*

to disarm the poor of their hostility toward the rich: it pre-
vents being poor. Agrarianism is the revenge of poverty
against wealth. The wanton destruction of the property of
others—the burning of hay-ricks, and corn-ricks, the dem-
olition of machinery because it supersedes hand-labor, the
sprinkling of vitriol on rich dresses—is only agrarianism
run mad. Education prevents both the revenge and the
madness. On the other hand, a fellow-feeling for one's class
or caste is the common instinct of hearts not wholly sunk
in selfish regard for a person or for a family. The spread of
education, by enlarging the cultivated class or caste, will
open a wider area over which the social feelings will ex-
pand; and, if this education should be universal and com-
plete, it would do more than all things else to obliterate
factitious distinctions in society.[7]

Education is seen as a means by which a society can function in a social and economic context. The interesting contrast
is that where biblical instruction focuses on the person and his
or her character, the thrust of public education is core skills tied
to functioning in society.

An exception to this goal of mass education is the liberal
arts school, where integration and character goals are important. John Henry Newman explained the goal of education this
way: "Education is a higher word; it implies an action upon our
mental nature, and the formation of character."[8]

Comparing Mann with Newman, we sense a different emphasis. Education limited to skills leaves the soul short. It limits
our appreciation of the value of the work that others do. Work
is about more than the paycheck. Work also takes teamwork.
Good education will not only mean good skills in reading, writing, and arithmetic. It will mean developing a social awareness

and discernment about being a contributing part of society, including issues of citizenship and social judgment. To do this well, children need to appreciate who they are and also who others, different from them, are.

Education limited to skills leaves the soul short.

BIBLICAL VALUES

While education in our recent past focused on group teaching across family lines, education in biblical times was tied to the home, although there are important exceptions. Still, the point from Scripture is that the home is where education and character development are reinforced.

Old Testament Examples

- Deuteronomy 6:6–9 has parents teaching their children the commandments of God. *"Teach [these commandments] to your children and speak of them as you sit in your house, as you walk along the road, as you lie down, and as you get up. You should tie them as a reminder on your forearm and fasten them as symbols on your forehead. Inscribe them on the doorframes of your houses and gates."*
- Proverbs 1–9 has the picture of a father teaching his son wisdom. Verse 8 says, *"Listen, my child, to the instruction from your father, and do not forsake the teaching from your mother."*

- Daniel 1:4: Daniel was raised as a faithful Jew, but also was instructed in Babylonian literature and language.
- Acts 7:22: A similar tradition of training beyond the home exists for Moses and Egypt: "*Moses was trained in all the wisdom of the Egyptians and was powerful in his words and deeds.*"

What the examples of Moses and Daniel show us is that, even in pious contexts, there was appreciation of the need to understand the world in which we live.

- Joseph: As a slave sold into captivity by his brothers, Joseph had to adapt to one new situation after another. But through it all, Joseph relied on God and was ultimately named second only to pharaoh as ruler of Egypt. What this shows is that functioning cross-culturally is a skill Scripture holds up as exemplary in some of its greatest heroes.

Insights from New Testament Teaching Style

Jesus' teaching and preaching—which was in the temple and synagogues rather than in homes—shows that religious instruction was tied to sermons and exhortations. Jesus extended such teaching to public settings, as did Paul.

- Matthew 5–7: Jesus gave the Sermon on the Mount for public instruction in the formal "sermon" style of the synagogue.
- Luke 4:14–30: In this synagogue speech, Jesus followed the formal custom, as he read from the scroll of Isaiah and then expounded upon it.
- Acts 13:16–41: When Paul addressed the synagogue in

Pisidean Antioch, he stood and preached a full-fledged sermon consisting of the history of the Israelite nation until that time.

Of course, these examples represent a more limited instruction than the range of courses in education today, but they confirm the value of education throughout biblical history. Beyond job skills, this instruction highlighted issues of character and living together.

EDUCATION IS ABOUT MORE THAN ACHIEVEMENT TESTS

I work in the area of education. I know about educational assessment and its role in a curriculum. Our seminary makes assessments in various ways. Some assessments measure raw knowledge; others measure skills. It is easier and far less helpful to measure only raw knowledge. Most national assessments look at raw knowledge.

It is easier and far less helpful
to measure only raw knowledge.

In assessing college readiness, David Conley named the following skills in two main areas.[9] Real assessment has to touch on all of this.

First, cognitive skills. Conley notes the importance of analysis and reasoning-argumentation-proof. Within those skills, the student must have:

- intellectual openness
- inquisitiveness
- interpretational skill
- precision and accuracy in dealing with the subject
- problem solving

Creating tests to measure these skills is not easy. Testing fact recollection is relatively straightforward in comparison to asking and showing how an argument is made or a problem solved. Most of our internal curricular measurements at the seminary fall in these more difficult areas, involving essays or direct individual assessment of oral presentations, like sermons. But for some of our larger assessments, we fall back into more straightforward multiple choice or fill-in-the-blank questions about core information. Argument assessment requires careful marking and feedback to help the student develop these abilities. These kinds of high-level assessments are not conducive to large-scale, national testing. They are too complex to mark efficiently and well in such numbers.

Second, academic knowledge and skills. These areas are more commonly assessed in national testing: core skills involve writing and research, as well as abilities in English, Math, Science, Social Studies, World Languages, and the Arts. These are the core academic areas of study; although in many contexts, the arts and languages get far less attention than the others. Many assessment tools in these areas involve multiple-choice exams, because they are more easily graded. Teachers will tell you these are often the least beneficial in measuring real student knowledge.

Beyond these two main areas named by David Conley, students need to be self-aware of who and where they are and have some level of self-monitoring and control—what we might call academic discipline or learning strategies—so they can do well.

While these skills do not test easily, they are core skills in working with others.

This listing shows that when meeting standards in national testing is the major goal of education, we are quite often majoring in the most rudimentary skills and levels—and these do not deliver all we really need to know. When performing well on standardized testing controls what is taught in the classroom, we not only fail to pursue real education, but we also make it harder to reach and assess the more advanced skills that really make up the core of genuine education. That kind of assessment is best done locally in the context of a reasonably sized classroom.

The objective here is not to do away with assessment. Good assessment is key to developing curricula. But really good assessment requires some level of teacher-student interaction where the factors impacting education are more knowable. Measuring the effectiveness of a school can still be done by examining how well the mass of a school's students do as they move on in education or in the businesses of life.

EDUCATION IS ABOUT MORE THAN THE KIND OF SCHOOL WE CHOOSE

A second concern is what kind of education we should support. The short answer is whatever forms prove to be effective.

Pursuing the Common Good

Having said this, it is important to recognize that all of us have a stake in how effective our entire educational system is. Educational policy is about more than my own child. The better the job we do in education, the better our workforce will be and the more competitive we will be as a people. So we want education to be effective no matter the institution or philosophy— whether public education, private schools, charter schools, or homeschooling.

The choice is about more than selecting the kind of school I want my child to attend. It is about pursuing the common good and showing concern for how all are educated. Thinking this way means that every school counts.

Developing an Understanding of People Who Think Differently

It's also important that education develop an individual's understanding about people who think differently and who value different things than I do. Learning to value others—especially those with whom we differ—prepares our children for the world they live in, not to mention that it equips them to come to the political table to converse openly and productively, especially about differences. When we live in a world that too often shuts off discourse on differences by dictating preordained responses, resentment builds up for those whose speech is throttled. This is one reason freedom of speech was seen as a core right at our country's founding.

Preparation for Jobs in a Globalized World

These thinking and communicating skills will also prepare students for the developments in jobs and skills surely to come in a globalized world. We need only think about what has happened to the job market in the last fifty years: whole new areas of employment have opened up as a result of the technological revolution and business innovation. We need to be prepared for whatever new jobs and ways of doing business may emerge.

Learning from Those Who Work the Closest with Students

As we all strive to improve our educational system, we need to be sure to honor the teacher-student relationship, much as we do the doctor-patient relationship. Teachers who work directly with students and administrators at their local schools will know more about the individuals they teach than those who look down from above—especially if they are professional and skilled at doing their jobs. Of course, teachers who show an *inability* to teach effectively need to be held accountable for not serving well the children we have entrusted to them. That said, there is much to learn from teachers who are in the classroom every day and have great insight into what is needed, what is working, and what is not.

We need to be sure to honor the teacher-student relationship, much as we do the doctor-patient relationship.

Why Parents Opt Out of Public School

There are many reasons parents decide to choose an alternative to public education.

Some of those reasons are:

1. *Safety:* Of course, safety needs to be a paramount value. Learning cannot take place when students fear bullying or other personal threats.

2. *Classroom effectiveness:* When their children aren't learning well—whether due to an inept teacher or a difficult classroom environment—parents often feel the need to find a better solution. And sometimes, there really are better solutions for certain families and students.

3. *Differing views on educational values and educational content:* Sometimes personal, family values seriously conflict with those of public schools. In such instances, each family needs to make their own decision.

But as we consider the above overarching concerns, we also need to consider the fact that public schools represent a variety of views in our society—and that can be a good thing. As a society—which begins with our children—we need to have awareness, appreciation, and respect for views, backgrounds, and people different from ourselves. Respect is not the same as agreement. Rather it is a recognition that differing ideas exist, and these ideas need to be contended for and shared in a world where people differ—without resorting to violence or demeaning. This is part of living in the world and a central part of education. Understanding this could sometimes convince parents to leave their children in public schools, as they might choose a value that enables their children to engage with the variety of views they will encounter in later life.

Socialization is a key part of what corporate education delivers. But sometimes options and alternatives need to be available to parents in some of the more sensitive areas of instruction, especially those that touch on values. This can be facilitated when parents are engaged with the school, and when the school is willing to be sensitive to the corporate concerns of parents. In most cases, however, education leans in the direction of exposure versus censorship.

Everything I have noted about education assumes involvement by the child's parent(s) or guardian(s). Part of the issue in the initial levels of education is that parental awareness and support often is not present. This lack of reinforcement impacts education. A teacher can only do so much with a child who is not his or hers. Education works best when such involvement takes place so that time spent doing homework and other out-of-class activities are meeting with encouragement.

Making decisions about preparing our children for a globalized world leads us into a final concern when it comes to education.

EDUCATION IS ABOUT MORE THAN FACTS AND SKILLS

The role of education in our society is about much more than teaching facts and skills—it's also about preparing students to function in an ever-changing world and with integrity and an understanding of our corporate citizenship.

Preparation to Live and Work in a Globalized World

Living and working in a globalized world means being able to function not only in our own society, but also in a mixture of global cultures. This means that our workforce needs to be nimble in thinking and interacting with others. It also means—as we've stated before—having some appreciation for the variety of religious and other, more secular values that exist across the globe.

Education can play an essential part in helping us understand values that are different from ours. By "understanding," we are not talking about changing our views to match those of others; neither are we talking about religious indoctrination. We also are not talking about being overly tolerant. Tolerance can masquerade as moral indifference when it ignores:

- real differences that do exist between religions
- the motivations for actions within various faiths

The fact is that even within a particular faith, there are important differences in approach. Again, this is not about endorsing a specific religious viewpoint. It is about understanding our global world. I grew up in a time when Judeo-Christian values were part of my schooling, but I was woefully unprepared for a world where people are also Buddhists, Hindus, Muslims, and believers in a myriad of other faiths or non-faiths. It became clear that I was not equipped to understand that people often reacted as they did because of their beliefs. Such knowledge is crucial—not so much as a matter of determining what or who is right or wrong—but in working hard to relate better to a neighbor who is different from me.

Preparation to Be a Person of Character

Our education also needs to discuss matters of *character*—core values like human dignity, honesty, integrity, the pursuit of virtue, and other elements of character development. When education is merely about skills and knowledge, we risk producing people with hollow souls and questionable character, who have little understanding of the core ideas that motivate their neighbors or the core skills that help us all relate to one another. When we focus chiefly on facts and skills, we leave the impression that who we are as people matters little. We risk getting what we pay for: people who can perform but may not do so with any large sense of civic or personal moral responsibility. In fact, we would argue that part of what we are facing today is the product of education where values lag or are left behind.

There is something to be said for the universality of teachings like the Ten Commandments and the Golden Rule. Most religious traditions, and many secular, embrace human relationships at the general level addressed in these teachings— teachings that affirm human dignity. Religions that see all of us as being made in God's image occupy a similar place. So, while we have a lot of differences, we can also find common ground, which can lead to the common good.

Preparation to Be a Better Citizen in a Corporate and Diverse Society

As we look at the choices we face as a society, we are sometimes hard-pressed to find a sense of corporate responsibility and cooperation. One of the burdens of this book is to argue that we need a better citizenship that asks a different set of questions as it faces the tensions and dilemmas in our world. We need a better level of conversation and debate. Citizenship means having an accurate sense of who our citizens are as a community and an appreciation of the communities that make up our nation. An education with depth will pursue such issues as children grow older. It will seek to produce people who are reflective about the world they live in beyond their own personal needs.

It will seek to produce people who are reflective about the world they live in beyond their own personal needs.

Teaching More Than the Common Core

There is much debate today about evaluation tools like the Common Core—a current effort to move toward a comprehensive curriculum and consistent standards. Seeking some level of shared standards for education is not an unworthy goal. Yet when we focus on these core knowledge areas, we may miss what makes humans tick from within. Another question is whether the common core really gets at what is common, or if it is slanted in directions that deserve much more debate and reflection on options. Once again we may be missing some questions we could and should be asking and some conversations we should be having with children as they grow up so that they are better prepared to have those conversations as adults. Failure to do so now while children are in school will mean failure later as well—when they are in the position of making decisions about how our society will function and why.

So . . . What Would Jesus Say about the Role of Education in Our Society?

Interestingly, much of the Bible can be viewed as educational. It is here that we learn who God is, who we are, how we are to relate to others, and where we are to take stands. We are even taught how we as humans are to relate to our physical environment—stewarding it well.

In the Old Testament passages we looked at, we saw a focus on education within the family. But we also saw instruction in the literature and language of other nations—as with Moses, Daniel, and Joseph. In the New Testament, we saw teaching in the public arena—specifically in synagogues. Both family and public education are valid and needed approaches.

As we consider the contrasts between biblical instruction and public education, we see that biblical instruction focuses on the person and character, while the thrust of public education is on core skills tied to functioning in society. However, we need to reflect on where values come from for children who do not have a home life that is stable and reinforces learning. To underestimate the importance of their education now means social trouble later.

While Jesus obviously focused on teachings about character, he also told several parables relating to wise and unwise business interactions. These business-related parables have application beyond business, and we can learn much from them. Just a quick look at some of his parables gives us principles we can apply to our conversation about education—related both to character and business.

Life's Work Application

- *Ensure that your life's work is built on a firm foundation and think ahead.* In the Parable of the Wise and Foolish Builders (Luke 6:46–49; 14:28–30), we see what happens when we don't look to the future as we begin a business effort and do not plan wisely. Jesus is discussing discipleship here and building on a moral foundation like he provides, but the example comes from work and planning in everyday life.
- *Be shrewd or think ahead in your business and life dealings to win friends and show yourself trustworthy.* The Parable of the Shrewd Manager is an interesting one (Luke 16:1–13). In a purely monetary business venture, the shrewd manager reduced the loans of his master's debtors so that

they would be his friends when the manager lost his job—
which was imminent. One of the lessons Jesus drew from
this was *"If then you haven't been trustworthy in handling
worldly wealth, who will entrust you with the true riches?"*

Character Application

- *Be proactive in coming to the aid of others—even when
  your personal values and heritage conflict with theirs.* The
  Parable of the Good Samaritan (Luke 10:25–37) is about
  two men whose national tendencies were to hate each
  other. The Jewish man was in need of help—but none of
  his fellow Jews who passed him on the road stopped. The
  only one who did help was a Samaritan—of a nationality that was hated by many Jewish people simply because
  they came from a different background. The hated "foreigner" was the hero in this story. He didn't hesitate to
  help an avowed enemy. Jesus was also reminding us that
  neighbors sometimes come in surprising packages.
- *Beware of greed.* In the Parable of the Rich Fool, we see
  that someone who might be considered a wise business-
  man was punished for being greedy with his earnings
  (Luke 12:13–21).
- *Be kind to the poor.* The Parable of the Rich Man and
  Lazarus paints a bleak picture of the eternal destiny of a
  rich man who turned a blind eye to a sick beggar (Luke
  16: 19–31; also 14:13).
- *Don't proudly rely on self-righteousness or religious heri-
  tage, when humility is what God wants.* The Parable of the
  Pharisee and the Tax Collector (Luke 18:9–14) portrays

a haughty Pharisee who falsely assumed that his reward would be based on his works in contrast to a humble man who recognized his own spiritual need—which was rooted in humility, forgiveness, and mercy. When we pridefully claim that our personal positions are based on our personal merit out of an excessive sense of self-righteousness, we sometimes rely on that heritage rather than being humble and open before God. The humility God wants helps us appreciate what it means to be forgiven and understand of the value of mercy.

- *Beware of entitlements and show concern for others.* A life lived with appreciation of mercy and forgiveness demands less from others and more from ourselves—including responsibility for ourselves and for our neighbors. Jesus said that the greatest among us is the one who serves (Mark 10:41–45). 1 Thessalonians 5:14–18 says, *"Be at peace among yourselves . . . admonish the undisciplined, comfort the discouraged, help the weak, be patient toward all. See that no one pays back evil for evil to anyone, but always pursue what is good for one another and for all. Always rejoice, constantly pray, in everything give thanks. For this is God's will for you in Christ Jesus."*

These are but a sampling of teachings from Jesus' parables (all from Luke) and other New Testament texts on community relationships that should shape our approach to conversations about how education is meant to prepare students for both living in a globalized world and being men and women of character.

Once again we see tensions that need balancing and serious conversation, not in polemic, as often happens, but in the pursuit of facing what certainly is a complex challenge: educating all our children effectively for a world in which they will compete with some sense of understanding of who they are and what they are facing. When it comes to education, we need to think beyond our own children and ask also what is best for all of us. We need to think about character and relating to one another, not just skills.

THERE WAS a time when the seemingly undeniable realities of life and culture provided support and even confirmation for what Christians understood to be true about sexual ethics. Those days have passed.

—STANTON L. JONES AND MARK A. YARHOUSE,
*HOMOSEXUALITY: THE USE OF SCIENTIFIC RESEARCH
IN THE CHURCH'S MORAL DEBATE*

12

The Family

Sexuality and Individual Rights

THE MORE things change, the more they do *not* stay the same. When we turn to issues of marriage and family, we see a full-blown cultural revolution not only in how marriage and the family are seen but in how they function in our society. We just observed the impact of family on education, but that is but one area of impact. We start with marriage and family because sex is not just about sex. It is about families (or the lack of them) as well. Looking at the impact of sexuality on families and society is something that matters to all of us. The quotation that introduces our chapter goes on to list descriptively many of the changes in the last several decades that affect our views of sexuality, marriage, and the family. Here is a shortened version of that list (with a few of my own additions):[1]

SOCIETAL CHANGES THAT AFFECT OUR VIEWS OF MARRIAGE, FAMILY, AND SEXUALITY

- Effective contraceptive methods, in some cases, have broken the bond between sexual acts, conception, family life, and parenting.
- Views on marriage have changed our views on sexuality: the expectation that marriage is permanent and the moral view that sex should be reserved for marriage are no longer prevalent in our society.
- Certain behaviors that were once described by a majority as deviant have become normalized and demystified for many.
- Urbanization and the rise of "sexual minorities" have emphasized individual liberty and entitlement as a means of popular affirmation and legitimization.
- Through the triumph of "essentialism," designations like "homosexual" are said to capture the essence of a person's self.
- Sexually titillating material is readily available at a click.
- In our sexually affirming culture, jokes about sexuality normalize once-off-limits lifestyles, and calls for restraint are seen as "puritanical."
- A change in tolerance levels of what used to be considered universally immoral has redefined claims about moral standards as patriarchal, imperialistic, or hateful.
- An escalating hostility toward the Bible and Christian tradition undermines the parameters for law, ethics, or virtue.
- Personal experience and desire override corporate societal impact.

- The rise of casual, multiple relationships in the hook-up generation further erodes the long-term commitment of marriage.
- The number of broken families and children raised in broken homes has weakened society as a whole and produced rising challenges for children.
- Because more and more people are identifying as transgender, what was once seen as a societal norm is now under contention.

Life in the twenty-first century is very different when it comes to marriage and family than it was even in my parents' generation. To discuss sexuality and family issues today in preparing pastors in seminary for ministry is very different than even a decade ago. It also is likely to be far different for my grandchildren's generation than it is for my generation.

The Effect of Births to Unmarried Mothers

The statistics listed below are tied to unmarried births as of 2011,[2] in an attempt to trace how things have changed since 1980.

A Timeline for Unmarried Births

In 1980, there were 29 births for every 1,000 unmarried women in the United States.

In 1994–2011, there were 46 births for every 1,000 unmarried women in the United States.

So the 2011 numbers represent a 59 percent increase since 1980.

In 2011, the rate of unmarried births for twenty to twenty-four year olds was 70 per 1,000, while for twenty-five to twenty-nine-year-olds, it was 69 per 1,000. The study points out that for twenty-somethings, the rate was almost 66 percent higher than the average in 1980. In 2011, three in ten women were in cohabitating relationships.

In 1980, 18.4 percent of all births were to unmarried mothers.

2009 had the highest percentage to date at 41 percent.

In 2010, nearly half of first births were to unmarried women of any age. In that same year, almost three-fourths of first births to women under the age of twenty-five were outside of marriage.

In 2011, that number was 40.7 percent, more than double the 1980 ratio.

Unmarried Births Fluctuate by Race or Ethnicity

Differences in the rate of unmarried births fluctuate widely by race or ethnicity when one looks at such statistics within a given group and compares them to one another. In 2011:

- 72 percent of births to black women only were outside of marriage.
- 66 percent of births to American Indian or Alaskan native women only were unmarried births.
- 53 percent of births to Hispanic women only were unmarried births.
- 29 percent of births to white women only were unmarried births.
- 17 percent of births to Asian or Pacific Islander women only were unmarried births.[3]

These family structures impact all of us. Here is what the childstats.gov report cited above said about the impact:

> *Children are at greater risk for adverse consequences when born to a single mother because the social, emotional, and financial resources available to the family may be limited. The proportion of births to unmarried women is useful for understanding the extent to which children born in a given year may be affected by any disadvantage—social, financial, or health—associated with being born outside of marriage. The change in the percentage of births to unmarried women reflects both changes in the birth rate for unmarried women relative to the birth rate for married women and changes in the percentage of women of childbearing age who are unmarried.*[4]

Societal Consequences of Non-Stable Homes

The revolution in views on family and marriage has brought huge social changes at significant social cost. The costs are not only present for any couple—married or not—but also for children who are brought into broken families, and for society at large, because of its impact in areas like education and social stability. Depending on sexual practices, sometimes individual and public health are at risk as well.

The revolution in views on family and marriage has brought huge social changes at significant social cost.

Marriage and families are important structures in our society. Broken homes and mixed marriage of all sorts exist. Children are impacted. Virtually all of us have been touched by the fallout from a divorce or a home where mutual respect between the parents or between parents (or stepparents) and children is lacking. Fully 30 percent of homes involve a nonbiological parent. Solid families are important elements to a stable society. The more stable families are, the better it is for society at large. The pursuit of virtue in our marital and family relationships is best for us all, whatever our laws are on these matters.

In sum, moral choices matter. As these children grow up under the pressure of a non-established home, they often fall into trouble and the consequences ripple across our society as a whole as we all pick up the pieces. The demise of the family in our culture is not good for us as a community.

A Secular-Sacred Divide: Free Choice versus Religious Concern

Freedom of Choice

On one side of this divide stands *freedom of choice*. But this freedom sometimes comes with a cost, and sometimes a significant one. It is here where freedom of choice cuts two ways: freedom of choice is a precious tenet of our society, but when we exercise that freedom without a sense of responsibility or restraint, we often get what we pay for. This is why freedom should come with reflection on what certain choices may mean.

As a society, we have the freedom to walk away from concerns about virtue and faith, but we might do well to consider what we get in exchange when sexuality becomes merely a product of free choice made in a non-moral, secularized environment. We can walk away from considering the impact of moral choices poorly made, but we will meet the consequences in the dysfunction that escalates in such environments. We can walk away from facing up to the results of such choices, but they do not walk away from us, as we meet them around the corner in the issues of the next generation.

Religious Concerns

On the other side stands a *religious concern* that holds to the merits of virtue and a sense of sacredness about marriage and family: the merit is that generally an intact home is healthy for the next generation of children and for society as a whole. When a solid sense of morality is pursued, the chances for kids and for our society improve as well. This is not to claim marriage is perfect—people are flawed and always will be. But the pursuit of virtue and honor in carrying a respect for others—as opposed to merely using them for our own pleasure or because of a convenient arrangement—reflects a love for our neighbor and serves the common good.

The Most Intimate of Relationships

Part of what we face in the secular-sacred divide is the impact of distinct worldviews. Ironically perhaps, with all the other issues we have discussed, there are ways through, and negotiating differences is quite possible. But when it comes to issues tied to marriage, family, children, and society—the most intimate relationships in life—the very proximity and quality, or lack of quality, in the relationships generates powerful consequences that are hard to avoid. In such areas, virtues matter and so do our choices. It is both the intimacy of these relationships and their importance in our personal lives that make this area one of such passionate debate.

This is why the church has in general been quite jealous to protect families and to discuss sexuality in the context of children and homes. Replacing sexuality in the context of home and family with the pursuit of pleasure—or even the right to love and regularly change "loves"—has reduced sexuality to a consumer product, shopped around and easily dispensed like a common can of soft drink.

Replacing sexuality in the context of home and family
with the pursuit of pleasure . . . has reduced sexuality to
a consumer product.

Intimacy has become something less than sacred or special. In its commonness, it is cheapened. The choice, which each of us has, has led to consequences that not only impact people when a child is kept in a non-established home, but also lead to other acts, like abortion. Abortion is a misguided attempt to obliterate the generational link that intimacy should create between those who "love" and the new life. After an abortion, the child may be gone, but the moment and choice are not easily forgotten.

Not about Can This Choice Be Made, but Should It Be Made

Our societal discussion here is *not* about denying someone the freedom to choose; it is about considering the cumulative impact and consequences of making those choices.

It is not about *can* this choice be made but *should* this choice be made.[5] This conversation is not about denying love to someone by saying you cannot love a specific person; it's about how that choice will affect society as a whole.

It is extremely relevant that both those inside and outside the church appreciate that the reason this topic is of such import is that our choices greatly affect familial and societal concerns. The personal nature of this topic is part of the reason it is so debated in large sectors of our society, in a wide array of areas touching marriage and the family—involving both heterosexual and homosexual relationships.

JESUS AND BIBLICAL VALUES

What the Bible Says about Intimacy and Marriage

Marriage virtually opens the Bible. And marriage, in the opening chapters of the Bible, reflects the gender variation in the Creation. In the beginning, God created a man and a woman—with different and complementary anatomies and different roles. Creation was not complete until both man and woman were created. In Genesis 2, the program for humanity was not complete until man and woman were paired. In both difference and unity, a bond showing how to relate to another who is very different from me was created.

- Genesis 1–2 presents Adam and Eve as the first couple to be married. The creation of woman completed the creation of humanity.
- Genesis 2:24 says, *"A man shall leave his father and mother and hold fast to his wife and they shall become one flesh"* (ESV). Here we see the creation of the home as the climax

of God's call to Adam and Eve to manage the world he had created. In Matthew 19:4–6 Jesus reaffirms this definition of marriage by citing Genesis 2 as he argues against divorce and for a stable marriage that honors its vows before God: *"They are no longer two, but one flesh. Therefore what God has joined together, let no one separate."* In these passages, marriage is seen as a sacred act where God joins together a man and a woman into a new social unit as a core structure in the creation. Family came before government.

Marriage is more than a temporary, mutually agreed-on arrangement. It forms a social bond picturing cooperation among the genders and standing at the base of society.

The sacred picture of that bond is reinforced when marriage is seen as a picture of Jesus' relationship to his church, with Jesus pictured as a groom and the church as the bride (Ephesians 5:22–33). This is why the church traditionally has been against divorce and why Jesus speaks strongly against it in Matthew 19 and in other texts, such as Matthew 5, Mark 10, and Luke 16.[6]

The family ideally was designed to be a stable place where children could be raised in an environment of affirmation and support.

- In Matthew 15:19, Jesus declared that among other things, sexual immorality defiles a person. It also damages the stability and trust that exists within a family. The Greek term *porneiai* is a broader term than adultery and looks to all kinds of sexual immorality outside of marriage. Jesus' standard for morality when it comes to sexuality appeals to its roots in the Torah. In the Old Testament, we see examples of polygamy, but the story is never a pleasant one.

Jealousy and trouble rage where partners are multiple. The story of Abraham, Sarah, and Hagar vividly shows this conflict. After years of trying to get pregnant, Abraham's wife, Sarah, told Abraham to sleep with her servant Hagar so that she could have a child on Sarah's behalf. But when Hagar became pregnant, jealousy and tension took over.

- By the time of the *New Testament*, monogamy is the standard—as church elders are to be the husband of one wife (1 Timothy 3:2).

The Old Testament addresses same-sex relationships as part of a larger list.

- In Leviticus 18, incest is rejected, as is adultery (another citizen's wife) and engaging in sex during a menstrual period (for reasons tied to Jewish uncleanness). These things are said to be *defiling*, using the same concept Jesus appealed to in Matthew 19. Leviticus 18:22–23, addressed to males, reads as follows, *"You must not have sexual intercourse with a male as one has sexual intercourse with a woman; it is a detestable act."*

Some people claim that same-sex marriage is not addressed in Scripture, but the above text addresses a same-sex act that a same-sex marriage would assume. The command never gets to marriage because the act behind it is treated first.

- In Romans 1:27–32, of the New Testament, a general rejection of same-sex sex is also affirmed by what Paul says. Here the apostle notes a full list of sins that leave all of us morally short—like covetousness, insolence, arrogance, and being gossips. Also in that list are same-sex acts. *"Men*

*also abandoned natural relations with women and were in-
flamed in their passions for one another. Men committed
shameless acts with men and received in themselves the due
penalty for their error."* Paul goes on to note that the problem is not only the choice to engage in such acts but giving approval to those who engage in such practices. When
Paul makes this point, he is speaking of the entire list he
gives, not just one particular sin. There are no greater and
lesser sins for Paul. Part of Paul's ultimate point is that, in
the pursuit of virtue and morality, we all fall short of God's
standards (Romans 3:10–18) and contribute to the ills of
our society. We all need his forgiveness offered through
the work of Jesus for our failure to live by divine moral
standards whatever those failures are (Romans 3:19–4:25).

Morality is something we must consciously pursue. We do
not get there instinctively. The challenge makes all of us accountable for helping humanity to flourish and pursuing the
common good.

What the Bible Says about Hatred

It is sometimes argued that questioning the morality of a same-
sex relationship is no different than questioning the rights of
women or the atrocities of slavery. In other words, some say,
Scripture is simply behind the times on these issues.

It is sometimes argued that questioning the morality of
a same-sex relationship is no different than questioning
the rights of women or the atrocities of slavery.

The question is an important one, as the argument is made that this way of life is a matter of human rights. Yes, God has given every individual the right to choose his or her way of life. No contest here. But if others suggest that choosing this lifestyle is against biblical standards, they are often viewed as hatemongers or racists. And yes, some individuals who oppose same-sex relationships are hateful and un-Christ-like in their behavior. But this does not change the fact that many who take this stand do so as a matter of conscience based on what they believe the Bible teaches and out of a genuine societal concern. They do so because they care about families, children, and society. They also have the same concerns for heterosexual failures in marriage and family.

For those who do mix hatred with their opposition to same-sex relationships, Jesus' words issue the following challenge: *"You have heard that it was said, 'Love your neighbor' and 'hate your enemy.' But I say to you, love your enemy and pray for those who persecute you"* (Matthew 5:43–44).

We are not saying that people who choose lifestyles that many people think are wrong are enemies; but if we are to love and pray for our enemies, how much more are we to love those who differ with us on this issue.

Yet the question remains, Is the issue of the freedom of sexual choice treated in the same way the Bible handles women and slavery? The Bible has many positive texts that elevate women and their spiritual giftedness (Luke 1:46–55; Acts 2:16–20; 21:9), and there are texts that talk about seeking freedom from slavery (1 Corinthians 7:20–24). However, there is not a single text in Scripture that views same-sex sexual contact in a neutral or positive light. Every mention is negative.[7]

This difference exists because sexuality, gender, and marriage are linked in Scripture. The power of sexuality is associated with its very intimacy as an act and the way it mirrors how we in general are anatomically created. Normally, sex is an exchange so intimate that it bonds people. This is why Paul argues that sex with a temple prostitute, which was an ancient form of casual sex, is a violation of the one flesh intention behind sexuality: *"Do you not know that your bodies are members of Christ? Should I take the members of Christ and make them members of a prostitute? Never!"* (1 Corinthians 6:15–16).

People exchange something intimate of themselves when they have sex. There is no such thing as casual sex when it comes to the soul. When it is treated casually, it offends the sacredness of the unique human exchange—whether that violation is heterosexual or homosexual.

So simply challenging same-sex relationships need not reflect hatred or an effort to control another's behavior and cancel his or her human right. People are free to act as they wish. We raise the issue to express a potential moral concern. The challenge raises legitimate questions about whether our free acts are best for us as individuals and as a society where we exist as male and female.

MARRIAGE, FAMILY, AND POLITICS

So what does all this discussion have to do with *laws* on marriage and family? Part of the goal of this section is to explain to those outside the church why this topic means so much to many in the church. The issue for many in the church is not about the freedom to act but about the individual and societal consequences of those actions. Our sexual choices actually have little to do with law and politics; but they have to do with personal and societal well-being. Those who choose otherwise, of course, are free to do so, but the choice may come with a cost to all of us.

Statistics on Stable Homes

Stable homes, however conceived, mean better results for children. It has long been recognized that children in two-parent homes generally do better than those not in such homes.[8] A 2009 study from Ohio State conducted by Claire Kamp Dush argued that a stable home—whether with one parent or two—increased the chances of a child's success.[9] The caveat here was that the statistic did not hold up for one-parent homes in the black community as well as it did in white and Hispanic communities. This may be because the additional family support structure beyond the parent is stronger in these communities. The study involved parents interviewed since 1979 and children aged five to fourteen in the years 1986–2004.

Statistics on Same-Sex Fidelity

In light of the statistics cited earlier on unmarried mothers and the above on stable homes, we now turn to statistics on same-sex marital/relational fidelity. The most famous study on this topic for marriages was released in 2010 by Colleen Hoff, professor of Sexuality Studies at San Francisco State. The press release summarizing this study says the following:

> *Hoff and colleagues surveyed 566 gay male couples in the San Francisco Bay Area and found that 99 percent had sexual agreements. Specifically, 45 percent had monogamous agreements, 47 percent had open agreements and 8 percent of couples had discrepant*

*agreements where partners reported a different under-
standing of whether they have an open or monogamous
agreement.*[10]

While the study did not trace the success of the agreements that
were monogamous, it did cover issues tied to HIV risk when
agreements are broken—urging a process by which the impact
could be assessed.

Here is a summary remark by Professor Hoff in the press
release: "Helping gay couples learn how to negotiate robust
sexual agreements and how to disclose and deal with a break
in an agreement could be an effective approach to HIV pre-
vention."

Perhaps the most cited study was led by Paul Van de Ven
from Macquarie University in Australia and chronicles that
most homosexual men have a significant number of multiple
partners.[11] Another study, covering 2002 and 2006–10, places
the mean level of male partners at two to three a year.[12]

These studies were carried out by people working to understand the relational dynamics in these kinds of relationships.
They took no moral view on these relationships, but merely ex-
amined their dynamics. The impact of this kind of relational
fluidity raises the societal concern.[13]

This chapter is not going to enter into the legality of same-
sex marriage. Given the mix in our society, it is not surprising
that the topic is a contentious one, even at the legal level. Many
people will respond to this issue at a worldview level—either
pro or con. Judgments also depend on how they see the human
rights and liberty issues that are tied to the discussion in relationship to their worldview.

Our society will continue to sort out what it collectively
thinks as the issue winds through various courts and legisla-

tures. The Obergefell decision—which ruled that the fundamental right to marry is guaranteed to same-sex couples—is now the law in our land for good or for ill. This raises first versus fourteenth amendment issues that will now be adjudicated for some time.

The goal of this part of the chapter has been to explain the societal concerns attached to this discussion and set them in a context that discusses marriage, whether one is speaking about heterosexual or homosexual relationships. Whatever route we take as a society, we cannot ignore the long-term impact of these choices. There is a case to be made here for the pursuit of virtue, even where choices exist.

Whatever route we take as a society, we cannot ignore
the long-term impact of these choices.

Biblical values affirming the cooperative roles of the genders and how they are called to work together is a major reason many reject same-sex marriage, even monogamous same-sex relationships. Same-sex marriage obscures the roles of various genders by its very one-sided nature. However, a reality is that these relationships exist in our society. We all need to figure out how we will live together in a society that permits such choices and gives such rights.

A FINAL WORD ABOUT RELIGIOUS CONSCIENCE

So there is one final issue that is a part of this discussion. It has to do with religious conscience and with personal practices that are seen as endorsements of something a person does not endorse. These involve legal cases tied to county clerks, florists, photographers, and cake bakers. In all these areas, same-sex couples asked for services that the business owner or government official viewed as an affirmation of the event, leading them to decline participation. That choice subjected the owner to legal sanctions and fines and sent a government official to jail.

Should People Be Punished for Following Their Consciences?

These examples are not raised to say the people in question made the right choice. They are raised to surface the question of whether we should fine people for carrying out an act of conscience in refusing to offer and be paid for services they do not feel morally comfortable rendering.

What if it were you being jailed for being asked to do something against your conscience? It is not as if there is a lack of other clerks, florists, photographers, or bakers who would willingly provide the service. Since the debate is about long-held convictions concerning actions that historically were not accepted, then shouldn't there be a place for an individual's conscience to be exercised?

One of the ironies of this discussion is that those seeking same-sex marriage argued that the restriction against it was oppressive to them and their lifestyle. Now that the tables are reversed, why should a similar restriction be applied in the opposite direction? Why not offer those who think differently the same personal space that was requested when the shoe was on the other foot? Can we learn from the past?

Shared Space: Sacred and Public

We also need some discussion of sacred and public space. I believe there is a way to be aware of and create space for both sides in this debate. Certain rights exist because people are human beings apart from the life choices they make. Having a livelihood, shelter, and food are basic rights that belong to all of us. In the public space, these core rights should be available to all law-abiding citizens.

Sacred space is a function of religious communities who desire to live by standards their faith has long accepted. This involves more than churches, synagogues, or mosques. Schools that offer religious training, religious organizations on college campuses, and relief organizations that operate as communities of faith—all seek to reflect the values of their faith and seek leadership that reflects those mutually affirmed values.

Religious liberty rights have always recognized that the conscience is a sacred space that ought not to be violated or coerced—as long the action of someone's conscience does not unduly burden another. Part of sorting out public space and sacred space is trying to be sensitive to the diversity in society that negotiates such shared yet sometimes contentious space.

Recent circumstances may ask us to rethink how we should react to this shared space. Should we punish a baker, florist, or photographer for that person's hesitation to see his or her craft as an affirmation of someone's else actions, when others would gladly offer the same service and join in the celebration? Is this an unduly burdensome option? On the other hand, does not a government worker take an oath that says he or she will uphold the laws of the land; and if there is nowhere else to get access to such service, should it not be provided? Should not that worker, if he or she objects, step aside and allow another to act in the worker's stead so that the government can give the service it says it will allow. Might there be ways for government to provide that service but not compel an individual person to act against his or her conscience? Such an option was created for conscientious objectors who were pacifists in terms of their belief about war. Can we think about something similar here?

Should we punish a baker, florist, or photographer for that person's hesitation to see his or her craft as an affirmation of someone else's actions?

The point is not an abstract one. Many religious communities will not be comfortable affirming same-sex relationships on religious, moral grounds, just as they question other practices by heterosexuals.

In thinking about public versus sacred space, can we consider the distinction between them? In parts of Europe today, to express one's convictions in this area is to be subject to hate-speech laws. Is this really what such speech is?

As we have tried to show, the discussion is not about hate but about society and, in some cases, long-held religious conviction. Hopefully we all can agree that there should be freedom of conscience in this area, as each side recognizes and respects the worldview elements in making judgments.

Now, someone may well think that the religious appeal to conscience is wrong and deserves challenge. Then let's have that exchange in vigorous public debate, not through legal sanctions, especially when a service is readily available from someone for whom providing it is not a problem. What was not good for the goose should not be forced on the gander.

Might we wrestle together with such distinctions in a way that might well affirm the need for legal protections on both sides of this divide? Could we accept that in public space full rights should be given, but that respect for conscience should be maintained in sacred communities? And can we not allow exemption from acts that can be seen as affirming services opposed by long-held religious standards and convictions important to the nature of that group or those individuals?[14] We do this in other areas of life, such as gambling or adult entertainment, where some view as acceptable what others regard as morally questionable. Might that kind of distinction apply here?

So . . . What Would Jesus Say about the Family and Individual Rights?

Few topics are as volatile as those involving the intimacy of relationships. And no wonder: God created us as relational beings. On the sixth day of creation, God created people in his own image. Genesis 1:27 says, *"God created humankind in his own image, in the image of God he created them, male and female he created them."* According to the Genesis account, God created male and female to complement each other, not work in isolation from each other. The family is a core structure of society that Scripture presents as a key feature to a stable society.

If our aim is to know what the Bible says about family, sexuality, and free choice, the following principles will guide our thinking:

- *God created humankind as two distinct sexes*—male and female.

- *When men have sexual intercourse with other men*, the Old Testament describes it as a "detestable" act (Leviticus 18:22–23).
- *Monogamy and sexual faithfulness are the standard of New Testament marriage* (1 Timothy 3:2).
- *Not a single biblical passage views same-sex contact in a neutral or positive light.*
- *Jesus is pictured as the groom and the church as his bride* (Ephesians 5:22–33). This sacred picture of Christ and the church is one of the reasons that, traditionally, the church has opposed divorce and honored the picture of marriage and the family.

As we, as a society, wrestle with these issues, let us allow room to contend for such choices, and let's give space to conscience in how we resolve to live together in light of our differences, knowing that we all are accountable for the choices we make.

WE CAN know from science what the embryo is, just as we know from embryo technology what can be done to and with it. But we can know from philosophically informed reasoning what is morally permissible to do to human embryos and how it is morally impermissible to treat them. Human-embryo ethics is, in this regard, no different from the ethics of our treatment of minorities or dependents. Human beings are capable of understanding, through reason, that it is morally wrong and unjust to discriminate against someone because he is of a different race or has a different ethnic heritage. And we are capable of understanding that it is wrong and unjust to discriminate against someone because of his age, size, stage of development, location, or condition of dependency.

—ROBERT D. GEORGE AND CHRISTOPHER TOLLEFSEN,
EMBRYO: A DEFENSE OF HUMAN LIFE, 2ND ED.

13

Abortion and Embryos

Right to Life or Right to Choose?

I F THERE is one issue that many think defines a religious versus a secular perspective on life and politics, it may be abortion and the associated activity that involves embryonic research. This, however, is misleading. It is true that there is a religious dimension to the arguments of many on this topic, as this chapter also will argue, but it is not a religious argument alone.

The case for preservation of human life operates at many levels, as the quotation opening this chapter notes. Moral arguments based on reason and the nature of science about the earliest stages of life can make a case for the embryo being a human worthy of moral and societal protection. Some atheists, such as Bernard Nathanson, have argued for fetal rights and pro-life options.[1] The George and Tollefsen book already noted is a careful scientific and philosophical look at the issue, while a work by Christopher Kaczor takes a close look at the moral argument.[2]

The reason this chapter is placed at the end of the book is that, just as concern for the common good and human flourishing throughout this book has led to respect for human life, the same core human and humanist concerns apply to this debate as well.

The moral worth of a human life, whether fully present or present in potential, makes the nature of the choice a moral one worthy of careful reflection, even where there is human freedom to abort. Legal freedom of choice and liberty to choose how our own bodies are used does not free us from the obligation to consider the morality involved in the choice.

The moral worth of a human life, whether fully present or present in potential, makes the nature of the choice a moral one worthy of careful reflection, even where there is human freedom to abort.

The pursuit of virtue—argued for as far back as Aristotle—shows that in discussing virtue, reason and religion can and should converge. The fact that there is convergence at multiple levels strengthens the case that the core choice is a moral one on behalf of human life. That convergence, as we hope to show, involves religious, human, and scientific considerations.

BIBLICAL VALUES ON THE ORIGIN OF LIFE

Recently Planned Parenthood made a claim that clerics and the Bible permit abortion. No texts were cited. The claim was made in a letter to offer comfort for those who sought to terminate pregnancies. It might be better to see what the texts actually say.

In an earlier chapter on starting points, we made the case

that the value of a human life and its sacredness are tied to people being made in the image of God. Humans have a capability for reflection and discernment that goes beyond other living species. This ability to manage and be creative is at the core of what a human is.

- Genesis 25:23: In this passage, life in the womb is affirmed when God tells Rebekah, *"Two nations are in your womb, and two peoples will be separated from within you."* Here, the yet unborn brothers, Jacob and Esau, are seen as the fathers of two nations, even while they are still developing in Rebekah's womb.
- Psalm 139:13 says, *"Certainly you made my mind and heart; you wove me together in my mother's womb."*
- Psalm 139:16 says that the psalmist's existence was spotted by God as he lay in his mother's womb: *"Your eyes saw me when I was inside the womb. All the days ordained for me were recorded in your scroll before one of them came into existence."*
- Jeremiah 1:5 says that the prophet was chosen from the womb.
- In Luke 1:41–43, the fetal John in Elizabeth's womb leaps for joy at the fetal Jesus' presence in Mary. Elizabeth is at least six months pregnant in this text, but Mary is portrayed as just having come to be with child.

Also revealing are the laws of Israel:

- Exodus 21:22: If a man strikes a pregnant woman and the baby survives, a monetary penalty—determined by the husband and agreed to by some form of civic council—is required. This makes the act a legal and civic affair. On the other hand, if there is injury, then the penalty is life for life, eye for eye, and tooth for tooth (vv. 23–24).[3] The value of the child and the offender are seen as equal by the law.

These texts argue that life forms in the womb and that equal rights apply to the fetus.

WHEN DOES LIFE BEGIN?

Both secular and religious people have recognized that life exists in a mature fetus. Such moral concerns explain why abortions in later trimesters have been illegal. A more complex and debated question is when life begins. Thinking about this question also raises the issue of the moral status of embryos. It is here that discussion enters into science.

The beginning of life has been variously defined scientifically. Opinions taking a view about the earliest onset of life run from saying it's the moment the sperm and egg fuse into what is called a zygote to describing it as the onset of gastrulation some two weeks later, as Maureen Condic does.[4] The formation of the zygote comes before implantation in the uterus, which comes five to six days after fertilization. Others opt for some form of viability independent of the mother's body, something technology makes a moving target, getting earlier and earlier. By any of these definitions, the formation of life comes very early, far before the time most abortions take place, not to mention any experimentation with cells in an embryo. However, this claim is not transparent and so is disputed, especially in the earliest period.

In the Condic article, the point is made that the embryo does *not* "develop" in a way analogous to manufacturing where additional ingredients are added along an assembly line to lead to the completion of the product. Rather, the article argues that growth is generated from within the embryo with material inherent in it. An embryo shows evidence of complex life from the start.[5] The point here is that an embryo that leads to life does not develop in the sense we tend to think about things being built. It is not a matter of growing to a point of sustainability and then reaching a separate point down the road when it is human. Its humanity is built in from the start. Granted, it is dependent on the mother's support for a time, but that is also true after birth, as mothers or parents still need to feed and care for their newborns.

It is not a matter of growing to a point of sustainability and then reaching a separate point down the road when it is human.

Everything said in the last two paragraphs describes the science of what is taking place in the womb. No ethical, moral, political, or religious question has been put in play by what has just been described.

In sum, one can argue that life begins when full life-generating processes are birthed into function. With that element in place from science, we can now raise the ethical questions that flow from it.

JUSTICE AND ETHICS: ON TREATING A HUMAN AS A HUMAN

As with every other chapter in this book, we have argued for a moral imperative to ask a full array of questions about human care and flourishing for the common good. In the case of a developing person, once life is in place, care and effort to preserve that life should be pursued to the fullest. One person's liberty is also concerned with another person's liberty. When there is a clash, that tension needs to be negotiated, not trumped with only one voice getting to act. This is one way of living with our neighbor responsibly, even when that neighbor is in the home of a womb.

The core question here is neither political nor religious. That is because we are discussing two persons—one of them unable to speak for his or her existence, even though that person's life is growing into maturity—a process that birth actually extends but does not initiate.

To argue for the ethical care of this growing being, and thus, for legally protecting it, is not the same as the government arbitrarily imposing itself into my business or seeking to enter into another's womb. Nor can the question merely be answered with cries about individual liberty. Neither is the argument merely one of religion, although religion does add a note about the sacredness of the life that is being nurtured into fullness.

In other words, if we seek to love our neighbors and to be concerned for virtue and human flourishing, then we will treat the life maturing within a womb with utmost care. We do this out of the pursuit of justice and because of the core ethics that value human life. We also do so with an ear to the one whom society often treats as hidden and therefore not relevant, because it still is a life even if it has no voice.

The situation is best summarized by a fifteen-year-old pregnant mom from New Zealand. Georgia Hageman saw her responsibility this way:

> *It does not matter if your world is falling apart and you feel that every day that goes by is getting worse. There is a life relying on you, and no matter who stares, who judges, who talks, the fact that you are staying strong for the child is a success. I do miss my old life sometimes, but my role in the world has changed and that's okay. It's no longer about me; it's about my gorgeous baby boy who I will be meeting in a few weeks. . . . He is the person I stayed strong for and fought for, and I will continue to do so. My age no longer matters. He needs me and that's what matters.*[6]

ANOTHER ISSUE WITH A REAL DIVIDE

Most of the issues treated in this book involve judgments about how to balance convictions that are very much in tension. Most chapters have argued that genuine discussion balancing the array of factors is needed. But this issue is an exception to that situation.

With an emerging life, the science and ethics converge on one side. What has made the issue so hard is that a decision for the life of the child produces a real and immense human burden for care of the newly conceived and born. This is a very real tension, but caring for a child is part of the responsibility of exercising our choices and pursuing virtue for a common good. Bearing a child is not a trivial commitment.

The sometimes burdensome factor of child care needs to be appreciated as we pursue a way forward, even as we recognize that those who are pro-choice sense the burden of this additional concern. Granted, some want simply to dispense with the burden and put it behind them, but many do not. They sincerely wrestle with the choices involved.

So we need to have a clear head about what is involved with the developing child and yet also possess a sensitivity to the dilemma some find themselves in. We as individuals must recognize that a newly formed embryo is life and needs protection. At the same time, we need to recognize a corporate responsibility to societal care if a mother is asked to bear a child under personal duress. We should encourage ways to care for both lives so that life is preserved—even when the mother senses or possesses a real burden in childbearing. When we encourage mothers to bear the new lives they hold, we also need to consider how to support those who may well need support.

So the divide about the presence of life versus a mother's choice to bear a child need not lead to an impasse. We have good moral reasons to ask and urge the mother to bear the burden for the nine months or so. Then, being open and creative, society at large can step in with compassion and do its part.

Many couples long to raise a child but cannot conceive themselves. Often those families go overseas to find a child. Why is that necessary? Why not make adoption of a child brought to term by a mother who otherwise might abort simple and relatively inexpensive? Why can't churches, synagogues, or other organizations set up ways to arrange for care of these children, including ultimate placement?

Imagine if Planned Parenthood actually helped people to plan for being parents who otherwise don't know how. But the irony of today's situation is that mandated health care includes abortion.

Promoting adoption is evidence of a society that cares about life and justice. It reveals a society that engages in the sacrifice and energy that often come with making good moral choices. In many areas of human life, we allow the pursuit of a corporate goal or value to trump our individual choices and freedoms. Why can't we do that with life or potential life?

Promoting adoption is evidence of a society
that cares about life and justice.

Whether we think of military service or forms of volunteer work, people give sacrificially for the good and protection of others. Some regularly go out of their way to rescue strangers whose lives are in danger. Such actions become stories of valor and elevate the person who stepped up as a hero.

Rather than insisting on a "right" that is morally questionable as an entitlement, why can't our society create paths that encourage taking the higher road? If we care about human flourishing in all the many other issues we have raised, why not also care about it here? Might this be another way through in an area that has been full of societal contentiousness?

COME LET US REASON TOGETHER

When a mother's health is at risk because of a pregnancy, we face a moral dilemma about the feasibility of abortion above adoption. In this case, the choice is between which life to preserve. The case of rape is also raised as another possible exception, but it is a more complicated category.[7]

Outside of these exceptional cases, the choice to abort is often cast as a choice between life and freedom. Usually life and freedom work together, but in this circumstance they are seen to clash. That need not be the case. If we are willing to pause and reflect on possible options, and if we as a society are willing to step in and be of help, then ethical choices can be made, lives can be saved and nurtured, and the burden on the child bearer can be minimized. As in any complex ethical choice, it is a question of will and sacrifice. It is a matter of loving your silent neighbor for the common good.

This is not an unreasonable option. As in many of the issues we have traced, there is no need for gridlock. What is needed is a reframing of the debate and a mutual openness from both sides to seek a solution that gives some space and relief toward those who see things differently. It is quite possible to get there together if we think together about other ways to solve this issue rather than focusing on our differences.

ABOUT EMBRYOS

Everything we have observed about the creation of life also impacts how we view embryos. As a moral matter growing out of the science of the origin of life, embryos are not mere raw pieces of indiscriminate tissue that simply go into a test tube to be manipulated however we wish. We are not merely harvesting biological matter. Developing humans are being violated—humans whose rights are being denied.

Once again we see the idea that because we are free to do

something, it does not mean we are moral in doing it. Of course, some maintain that an abortion can benefit the life of the mother. But taking one person's life simply at the convenience for another when both can be preserved is not a moral act. We can do better as a people than to use claims of liberty to deny liberty to someone who is not able to defend him- or herself.

So . . . What Would Jesus Say about the Value of Life?

Life is precious, even developing life. Life at such a tender stage needs more protection, not less.

From the principles taught in Scripture, we glean the following truths:

- *Human life is valuable because all people are created in the image of God.*
- *God recognizes life as beginning in the womb* (Genesis 25:23; Psalm 139:13, 16; Jeremiah 1:5; Luke 1:41–43).
- *The life of an unborn child is as valuable as a grown man's.* Under the Old Testament law, when a pregnant woman was hit by a man and the baby died as a result, the "eye for an eye" guideline was employed (Exodus 21:22–24).
- *Caring for orphans (which some babies can be considered after they are born) is of high value to God: "Pure and undefiled religion before God the Father is this: to care for orphans and widows in their misfortune and to keep oneself unstained by the world"* (James 1:27).
- *We are to love our neighbors as we love ourselves.* Jesus said that loving our neighbor is the second greatest command

of all. The first being to love God wholeheartedly. *"The second is like it: 'Love your neighbor as yourself.' All the law and the prophets depend on these two commandments"* (Matthew 22:37–40). If we or one of our children were in need of care, we would provide that care without hesitation. But when Jesus told us to love our neighbors as ourselves, he was talking about helping any and all who are in need of help.

If we seek to protect all life sensitively, we can protect the unborn and provide a place for them once they are born that will give them a chance to succeed in life. When a child is adopted, not only is life preserved but the common good is served. It also shows a concern for all of life, from the unborn through to death.

Adoption may require short-term sacrifice for the mother while others step in to help long-term, but the result is developing a culture where all of life is honored and treated with the sanctity human life deserves. Adoption reflects a true and deep love for our neighbor. It is being humane in the best sense of the term. It is a choice we should make when we wrestle with liberty and life.

Give them liberty, give them life.

Engagement, Respect, and Loving Your Neighbor

T HE PURSUIT of the common good, at least in part, is about pursuing virtue in our society. However, pursuing the common good must also balance the diversity that is in our society. Virtue is about the balance between liberty and good choices. It is about judgments, both individual and corporate.

I may be free to choose to do all kinds of things. I may even have those rights, but that does not mean that everything I am free to choose yields good results. As Paul said, *"'All things are lawful for me'—but not everything is beneficial"* (1 Corinthians 6:12). God gave Adam and Eve the freedom to choose to eat of the tree of good and evil, but the choice to eat that fruit was not good and came with consequences. In both biblical passages noted above there is a lesson.

The legal right or liberty to do something does not mean it will be a right choice. Corporate human flourishing and the pursuit of the common good require that we reframe many of the issues we debate and see them in light of core questions about humanity—as special creatures in the creation. We are contending that, for the most part, our current politics fails to wrestle with the moral factors that these life tensions require. As some of our Founding Fathers showed in the quotations that opened our book, or as a well-known figure like William Wilberforce's life proved as he argued for an end to slavery, the wedding of politics and religious reflection can do our society good and contribute to human flourishing.

The legal right or liberty to do something does not mean it will be a right choice.

Getting out of gridlock requires a certain style of engagement, doing a better job of listening and balancing tensions versus pitting them against one another. Perhaps one of the reasons we are in gridlock is that our style of engagement leads into it. We do get what we pay for by how we engage. Unless we alter the way we debate and engage one another, little will change and all of us will continue to live in a world of gridlock, distrust, and hostility.

THREE OBSTACLES TO HELPFUL POLITICAL ENGAGEMENT

1. Niche Broadcasting

The first of three major problems in getting to solid political dialogue is the presence and success of niche broadcasting on political events on cable and over the web. Juan Williams, a political analyst for FOX News, pointed to this as a problem and called it narrowcasting, not broadcasting. It is a problem on both ends of the ideological divide. Whether we think of news organizations that favor the right or the left, the effect of these stations is not only a filter for the news, but a mostly one-sided framing of issues that never lets us really understand what the other side might be saying that could be of value. The pounding away at our leaders, of any political stripe, who hold views different from mine, almost always seeing the worst of motives for why they act, is a poison in our body politic.

Ironically, it matters little who or which party is in the White House, the other side will pound away at the credibility of the one in office. Airtime for the variety of points of view or the complexity of some issues is not in any kind of balance. Sometimes the worst of rumors are circulated.

My email inbox has managed to get one-sided mailings regularly—from each end of the spectrum. The result of one-sided listening, so prominent in niche broadcasting, is an increasing distrust of one another and a polarization of our politics. The monophonic sound each of these channels produces rarely leads to an understanding of the tensions we have discussed, much less any appreciation for them.

We simply choose sides and treat any form of discussion and compromise as a defection of loyalty—where everything worth defending is almost always said to be at stake. A fellow American becomes an enemy to be fought, not a neighbor to be respected.

2. Vilification of the Person Who Differs

The second obstacle, which has already been alluded to, is the vilifying of the person who holds different views. The attack is on the person's character or integrity rather than the substance of the issues. This is often done in sound bite form. This sloganeering approach to politics undercuts working hard at getting into the details of issues. If I can label opponents as socialists or fundamentalists, others of my persuasion will jump on the bandwagon with what they think is immediate understanding of where the person is coming from and why the person argues as he or she does. If I dress the opponent in black, then there is no need to listen to any reasoning about why things might be seen in a certain way.

Just look at some of the issue framing we have had in the last few years. Regarding the Supreme Court decision on Hobby Lobby, we heard that our bosses "determine our personal health care decisions." The justices who wrote on one side of the case are called "the Operatives."

On the other hand, when an ambassador at a US foreign embassy was killed by terrorist murderers, government leaders were accused of not caring about those who died. The more inhumane we can make the opponent, the less we need to take the opponent seriously—and the more money we can raise for our cause.

On immigration, people who want leniency do nothing but "support lawbreakers and criminals"; while those who want tighter regulations are portrayed as racist or heartless because they only care about the rule of law. Do these labels really advance the substantive discussion we need to have on a topic where both sets of concerns are legitimate?

We accuse our president of seeking to be a king when he unilaterally acts on legislation that is never even put on the docket for a vote, after long committee study, yet one person on the other side in Congress can determine by him- or herself whether a vote, which most legislators may support, can even come up for a decision. Who acts as a king then?

My point is that both sides are equally guilty here. This rhet-oric and framing of the issues, this constant posturing for po-litical advantage and the campaign dollar, does little for us than preach to the choir and make it more difficult not only to have a necessary conversation but also to hammer out options that we need to consider.

Both sides are equally guilty here.

---

3. Special Interest Money Influences Politicians

The third obstacle involves the vast amounts of money used to frame all of this rhetoric, making the politicians beholden to special interest groups. Politicians are so busy chasing their next campaign dollar that they don't think about what is best for the country. They end up serving the special interests that fund them versus the people who elected them or all the peo-ple they represent. The average person has no chance of being elected today without the support of a number of kingmakers. The tension here is that our system promotes involvement and does not restrict it. Freedom of speech allows for this kind of activity, so it becomes the responsibility of citizens and infor-mational professionals (the media) to do a better job of gate-keeping here.

My ultimate point is that we get what we pay for when we allow these structures to dominate our political landscape. As citizens, we are responsible to counteract them by engaging re-sponsibly in the choices that are ultimately in the hands of the people. It requires we be good citizens who are engaged and well informed, committed to hearing all side of the debate. Unless we get past political vilification, candidate dependency on special interest dollars, and selective hearing on the issues, we may be doomed to live in a country so divided it remains significantly dysfunctional.

The Problem of Affordability

Another very real issue is affordability. It takes significant funding to engage in corporate care for people. The way we currently handle our budget makes no sense. During the one of the latest government funding crises, which temporarily shut down the government, we repeated a mistake we often make. When we looked at our budget, we left out of the discussion our largest areas of expenditure: defense, health care, and pensions. These three areas make up about 75 percent of our budget; and when they are untouchable, there is not much room for fiscal maneuvering. Do we work harder to fund these programs, or do we cut them back to levels we can afford? Either way, how we collect our taxes will obviously be impacted.

No one likes taxes, but we do understand why we have them as we pursue goals that make for the common good. One way to get our minds around this issue is to compare where our tax structure falls in comparison with that of other industrialized countries. Out of thirty-four countries listed in 2013, the United States combined state and federal tax rate was 44 percent, placing it as the twentieth highest out of the thirty-four.[1] Denmark was the highest at 60 percent with Sweden next as 57 percent. The countries below us were Korea, Switzerland, Luxembourg, Slovenia, Norway, Chile, Turkey, New Zealand, Poland, Mexico, Estonia, the Slovak Republic, Hungary, and the Czech Republic. Above us in tax burden are countries like Japan, Austria, and the UK. They all sit at 50 percent. Israel, Canada, and Australia are at 48 percent.[2]

Another factor here is that higher rates kick in later for some than for others. In the United States a person has to earn roughly more than $400,300 before his or her high rates kick in as compared to $221,400 in the UK, $115,700 in Australia, $96,400 in Austria, or $54,900 in Denmark.[3] Only three countries—Spain ($430,300), Korea ($420,500), and Canada (409,700)—kick in at a higher rate than the United States. Even if we add in other factors, such as distinct costs of living or the value of distinct currencies, there is a significant difference here.

So obviously, one of our choices is figuring out how to pay for what we seek to do:

- How much should we sacrifice as individuals to seek to care for our larger society's needs?
- Do we do less or pay more?
- How much freedom should we give those at the top of the economic ladder to generate economic opportunity?
- Is the way we incentivize investment and corporations to generate more opportunity worth the loss of revenue?
- How should we balance incentivizing versus each group sharing the load?

It is hard to know how we can realistically meet our commitments without considering how our tax structure works at all its levels. But if much of this conversation is untouchable, pro or con, in terms of government involvement and affordable tax rates, then we box ourselves in and can never hope to get to any kind of resolution. When we add in the special interests at work to preserve existing protections, then we can see how we've set ourselves up for gridlock and being overextended.

Leadership would say we have to face up to our tax and revenue policies in order to sort this situation out. That observation applies to both sides of the aisle. Hard lines drawn on either side of the ideological divide mean we go nowhere. All-or-nothing approaches (more government care and taxes versus less taxes and less care) or suggestions that the private sector meet many of these needs are an oversimplification of the problem—especially in light of that sector's less-than-stellar track record (see its history on health care).

These are not simple or easy conversations. They involve wrestling with priorities and balancing competing interests, including those between the private and public sector. The least responsible thing we can do is to keep pushing the ball down the road and delaying facing what has been building up for decades. Blocking votes and the one-sided nature of our conversations—which lead to obstructionism or the use of unilateral acts—do not advance our cause.

Our legislature needs to put legislation on the table and vote on our priorities, based on the representative government we as people have sent to Washington. Corrections in direction are supposed to come when we elect those officials. We need to get to where we can pay for what we agree to do and show the appropriate self-sacrifice, or else scale back what we do to where we can afford it.

WHAT ALL OF THIS ASSUMES

The foundation of making our government and society function well is that we as citizens be informed and participate. Good citizenship means wrestling hard with how we can function well together—despite the many differences that exist in our diverse society. Positive citizenship means thinking about the common good, not just what's good for me. It involves wrestling with differences and being sensitive to living well with my neighbor. It requires listening, not belittling.

Good citizenship means wrestling hard with how we can function well together—despite the many differences that exist in our diverse society.

Life, Liberty, and Loving Our Neighbors

Throughout this book, we have been considering life—life as precious, life as sacred, and life as full of competing choices. We've raised questions about life where the common good is pursued, where life is honored, and where virtue is pursued—even in the midst of precious freedoms. When we pursue the common good, our neighbor often will be loved.

When we ask how Jesus would have voted, we are not speaking about choosing a specific policy but about having fruitful conversations that are helpful and in the right tone.

We take this path not because we agree on how each of us will pursue life and liberty, but because we are human and because virtue matters. We give space to people who think differently so we can figure out how we can best be neighbors. If we consider biblical values and what Jesus taught, then we go this way because we should appreciate that people are made in the image of God, that there is something sacred about life, and that everyone is worthy of respect—even in the disagreement and passionate debate about the direction of life and our society. We also know that when we use our freedom to make choices, we will sometimes choose well and sometimes choose poorly.

Freedom does not mean good choices are always made. It is one thing to have the freedom to choose something; it is another to choose well. Freedom can be suicidal or beneficial, depending on what the freedom to choose yields. So we should lift up freedom, but do so with an eye to being discerning about it. That is why we debate our differences and engage.

For those who see a world where God exists, part of our faith is that God will one day render true justice, and we will each be accountable for the good and bad choices we have made. In the meantime, the world will be an imperfect place, full of the tensions and balancing judgments, because humans are not perfect beings. If we do not treasure the sacredness of life, if we do not recognize that we are accountable to God for the choices we make, then each of us will have a tendency only to defend our own turf, and a very divisive gridlock will be all that remains. Unless each of us appreciates that we are all commonly human and need to look beyond ourselves, there can be no grappling to find the common good.

So . . . how would Jesus vote? His ballot would be cast for that which honors God and allows his creatures to flourish in life and to manage the creation well. His party would pursue the virtue that makes for a stable society and respects that we are all made in God's image. His approach would be to woo the one on the other side to consider a better, more virtuous path. Jesus' vote would not be to create people who function as independents but to have us sincerely seek the path that honors God and his creation. The mutual pursuit of that kind of common good would be good for us all.

NOTES

READER: Sources for chapter epigraphs are listed as unnumbered endnotes below, immediately following the relevant chapter heading.

INTRODUCTION

Ross Douthat, *Bad Religion: How We Became a Nation of Heretics* (New York: Free Press, 2012), prologue.

1. Juan Williams and Kenneth Starr brilliantly summarize this situation online at Ken Starr's *On Topic* as Williams discusses gridlock in Washington and what he calls narrowcasting instead of broadcasting. Narrowcasting is presenting the news from one point of view alone. See http://www.baylor.edu/president/index.php?id=862862. See minutes 12:36–21:38. Williams also discusses this issue in his book pleading for real public dialogue, *Muzzled: The Assault on Honest Debate* (New York: Crown Publishers, 2011).

CHAPTER I—HOW IT ALL BEGAN: THE PRINCIPLES THAT BUILT AMERICA

1. Michael Novak, *On Two Wings: Humble Faith and Common Sense at the American Founding* (San Francisco: Encounter Books, 2002).

2. On how this idea emerged, see Greg Forster, *The Contested Public Square: The Crisis of Christianity and Politics* (Downers Grove, IL: InterVarsity Press Academic, 2008), chapter 6. For a solid look at the history of religious liberty and the varying ways it has been treated in US history, see Steven D. Smith, *The Rise and Decline of American Religious Freedom* (Cambridge, MA: Harvard University Press, 2014).

3. Steven D. Smith, *The Rise and Decline of American Religious Freedom*, especially chapter 3. Smith argues that the series of decisions undercut a "valuable strategy for maintaining unity amid diversity" (loc. 2164). To elevate one approach to constitutional orthodoxy when both have claims to deep roots in American political tradition undercuts the "genius of the American Settlement" (loc. 2236). In this move, Smith argues the Court "unlearned the lesson Americans had taken from the religious strife that had afflicted post–Reformation Europe" (loc. 2553). Smith's description echoes Novak's *On Two Wings*.

4. John Adams expressed this call to rights for the people on both philosophical and theological grounds in an appeal to their being granted simply because people were human. He said, "Let us delineate before us the true map of man. Let us hear the dignity of his nature, and the noble rank he holds among the works of God,—and that God Almighty has promulgated from heaven, liberty, peace, and good will to man." He also stated a philosophical ground: "Let it be known, that British liberties are not the grants of prices of parliaments, but original rights, conditions of original contracts. . . . Let them search for the foundations of British laws and government in the frame of human nature, in the constitution of the intellectual and moral world." In the appeal to an "intellectual and moral world," Adams appealed to grounding in moral excellence, or virtue. By juxtaposing rights from God and rights that appeal to virtue in the same argument, Adams was arguing that virtue is grounded in a connection with the transcendent values that come from God, values Adams placed in the revelation from God. These two citations can be found in John Adams, "A Dissertation on Canon and Feudal Law," in George W. Carey, ed., *The Political Writings of John Adams* (Washington, DC: Regnery Publishing, 2000), 19.

5. James Madison, Speech to Congress, June 8, 1789.

CHAPTER 2—STARTING POINTS:
LOVING YOUR NEIGHBOR

Miroslav Volf, *A Public Faith: How Followers of Christ Should Serve the Common Good* (Grand Rapids, MI: Brazos Press, 2011), 77.

1. The speech in which this expression appears is particularly melancholic. It starts, "All the world's a stage, And all the men and women merely players. They have their exits and their entrances." It ends with a note about old age, "Last scene of all, that ends this strange eventful history, is second childishness and mere oblivion, sans teeth, sans eyes, sans taste, sans everything." If we come and we go in life as a bit player, no wonder so many people wrestle with purpose and direction, with a sense of alienation, loneliness, and depression as the result.

2. I do not plan a full chapter on issues of the environment. It also has tended to split along conservative and liberal lines. But the point here makes it clear that managing the creation well and caring for it is part of humanity's stewardship. To damage or destroy the creation we are gifted to live in is not responsible stewardship. So one should take seriously how we handle resources in such a way that we do not unduly damage the environment or ruin the creation for our children. The values represented here are nicely and succinctly stated in this document from the Lausanne's Global consultation on Creation Care—A Call to Action: http://www.lausanne.org/en/documents/all/2012-creation-care/1881-call-to-action.html.

3. Os Guinness, *A Free People's Suicide* (Downers Grove, IL: InterVarsity Press, 2012).

4. Ibid., 19.

CHAPTER 3—STARTING POINTS:
BIG GOVERNMENT OR SMALL?

Os Guinness, *A Free People's Suicide* (Downers Grove, IL: InterVarsity Press, 2012), 21–22.

1. Ancient texts reflect an awareness of the need to have such values. Human instincts have long applauded such concern. For the first-century

Jewish community at Qumran, see 1QS 5:1–3, 9:3–11. (1QS is also known as the *Rule of the Community*). The call here is to have a community that discusses law, money, and judgment. They are to practice the truth with humility. The Greek examples are presented by Plato (*Republic* 5.449C; *Critias* 110 C–D) and Aristotle (*Nicomachaen Ethics* 1168B: "Friends have one soul between them"). The idea here is we share life and its results together.

2. James Skillen, *The Good of Politics* (Grand Rapids, MI: Baker Academic, 2014), 128–29.

3. Michael Tanner, "Why the Size of Government Matters," *National Review*, March 20, 2013 (http://www.nationalreview.com/articles/343419/why-size-government-matters-michael-tanner). The citations from Tanner in this section of the discussion are from this article.

4. Douglas J. Amy, "A Guide to Rebutting Right-Wing Criticisms of Government" (http://www.governmentisgood.com/feature.php?fid=14).

5. This is a variation of the affordability argument. The question about the affordability argument simply asks if we can afford the service we provide or is the debt/sacrifice incurred worth the benefit provided. The affordability argument is usually asked as a way to say we cannot afford to offer such a service or entitlement.

CHAPTER 4—ECONOMICS AND POVERTY: PERSONAL WEALTH OR SHARED RESOURCES?

Austin Hill, and Scott Rae, *The Virtues of Capitalism* (Chicago: Northfield Publishing, 2010), 25, 37.

1. James Halteman and Edd Noell, *Reckoning with Markets: Moral Reflections in Economics* (Oxford University Press, 2012), especially chapters 2 and 3.

2. Wong and Rae, *Business for the Common Good*, 117–22.

3. Edd Noell, Stephen Smith, and Bruce Webb, *Economic Growth: Unleashing the Potential of Human Flourishing* (Washington, DC: AEI Press, 2013).

4. When we discuss capitalism, it is important to note that there are at least four kinds of capitalism: state-guided, oligarchic, big-firm, and entrepreneurial. This warns us to be careful not to generalize when

speaking about capitalism, or socialism, or a "mixed economy" such as welfare states today. What type of economy are we considering? What country provides the model economy? Is it the United States, the United Kingdom, Germany, Sweden, Japan, China, Russia, or another country? There is a spectrum of options, not just one model or one "pure" model. Does the type or some type of hybrid of the types make a difference for the strengths or weaknesses of what it can deliver? As in many of the areas we are discussing in this book, buzzwords and sound bites alone do not help us much. Nuance and detail can make a difference. Reasoned discussion is what we need, not class warfare. Kathryn Blanchard, *The Protestant Ethic or the Spirit of Capitalism: Christians, Freedom, and Free Markets* (Eugene, OR: Cascade, 2010), 218.

5. Steve Corbett and Brian Fikkert, *When Helping Hurts: How to Alleviate Poverty without Hurting the Poor*, (Chicago: Moody Press, 2009).

6. Ibid., 100.

CHAPTER 5—HEALTH CARE: COMPREHENSIVE COVERAGE OR CHOICE?

T. R. Reid, *The Healing of America: A Global Quest for Better, Cheaper, and Fairer Health Care* (New York: Penguin Books, 2010), 3–4.

1. Cochran and Kenney, *The Doctor Crisis* (New York: Public Affairs, 2014), 17.

2. Reid, *The Healing of America*.

3. Ibid., 9.

4. Ibid., 31–34.

5. Ezekiel J. Emanuel, *Reinventing American Health Care: How the Afford-able Care Act Will Improve Our Terribly Complex, Blatantly Unjust, Out-rageously Expensive, Grossly Inefficient, Error Prone System* (New York: Public Affairs, 2014), 100.

6. http://www.commonwealthfund.org/publications/fund-reports/2014 /jun/mirror-mirror. The source of this study is K. Davis, K. Stemikis,

D. Squires, and C. Schoen, *Mirror, Mirror on the Wall: How the Performance of the U. S. Health Care System Compares Internationally. 2014 Update* (New York: The Commonwealth Fund, June 2014).

7. Emanuel, *Reinventing American Health Care*, 102.

8. Reid, *The Healing of America*, 35, who notes that Texas has the toughest caps on malpractice in the country and yet health costs in the state are going up faster than the national average.

9. Ibid., 35–44. Reid's discussion supplies the statistics for this entire section.

10. A report from the Evangelical Free Church of America allocates 10 percent for administration of missionaries (http://go.efca.org/sites/default /files/resources/docs/2013/05/understanding-missionary-support.pdf). Cru says 12 percent of support covers two areas: administrative support and backup in areas where support raising is difficult to develop (http:// go.efca.org/sites/default/files/resources/docs/2013/05/understanding -missionary-support.pdf).

11. The claim that IUDs do not lead to potential abortive results, as articles in the *New York Times* claimed, selectively cites what the science shows. For the *Times* article, see Adam Liptak, "Birth Control Order Deepens Divide Among Justices," http://www.nytimes.com/2014/07 /04/us/politics/supreme-court-order-suspends-contraception-rule-for -christian-college.html?hp&action=click&pgtype=Homepage&version =LedeSum&module=first-column-region&region=top-news&WT.nav =top-news. For science arguing otherwise, see The ESHRE Capri Workshop Group, "Intrauterine Devices and Intrauterine Systems," *Human Reproduction Update* 14 (2008): 197–208, especially 199–201. This article has a full bibliography at the end. The percentage of incidence is not high, but it does exist. For this discussion, see Joseph B. Stanford and Rafael T. Mikolajczyk, "Mechanisms of Action of Intrauterine Devices: Update and Estimation of Postfertilzation Effects," *American Journal of Obstetrics and Gynecology* 187 (2002): 1699–708.

12. For a newspaper report on how this is viewed by a university also challenging the government position, see Tom Howell, Jr., "Religious University Balks at 'Accommodation,' Re-files Suit over Obamacare's Contraception Mandate," http://www.washingtontimes.com/news/2013 /aug/7/religious-university-balks-accommodation-re-files-/.

13. The scientific, moral, ethical, and religious rationales for this view are discussed in chapter 12.

14. For example, an opinion piece in the *New York Times* by Linda Greenhouse, "A Religious Case Too Far for the Supreme Court?" July 23, 2015, argues that the "opt out" form should be enough to satisfy religious organizations on being shielded from participation in providing the mandated care that is morally objectionable (http://www.nytimes.com /2015/07/23/opinion/linda-greenhouse-religion-case-too-far-for-the -supreme-court.html?ref=opinion&_r=0). But the very fact that one has to "qualify" and submit to an accommodation that reverts back to the institution's plan is also an issue here. What the courts are now debating is whether the submission of the form makes for an unreasonable burden on these organizations. Rulings involving Wheaton College and the Little Sisters of the Poor, among other cases at the circuit court level in 2015, have argued such an act is not a substantial burden, which is the technical legal standard being applied in such cases. The main contentions in the case for those challenging the government are the ideas (1) of qualifying for exemption through the accommodation form and (2) that this form simply reverts to the institution's plan for the provisions of care. The positive in this is that the form permits a self-certification of the claim. But the fact that the government even asks for it from a seminary or religious school or college is part of the religious liberty issue. Why should they have to certify this is what they are if their orientation is clear? The relevant 2015 cases are *Little Sisters of the Poor v. Burwell* and *Wheaton College v. Burwell*. For the issues they raise the cases are now combined on the Supreme Court docket for 2016. For a balanced summary of these issues legally and morally, dealing directly with some overreactions by those who disliked this decision, see Megan McArdel, "Answers to All Your Hobby Lobby Questions," *Bloomberg View*, July 2, 2014, http://www.bloombergview.com/articles/2014-07-02/answers-to -all-your-hobby-lobby-questions.

15. Making this point and showing its cultural value is one of the strengths of Steven D. Smith's *The Rise and Decline of American Religious Freedom*.

CHAPTER 6—IMMIGRATION:
THE CHARACTER OF A SOCIETY

M. Daniel Carroll-Rodas, *Christians at the Border: Immigration, Church & the Bible* (Grand Rapids, MI: Baker, 2013), 129.

1. Tim Keller, *Generous Justice* (New York: Penguin Books, 2010), 4, 194; Nicholas Wolterstorff, "A Contest of Nations," in his *Justice: Rights and Wrongs* (Princeton University Press, 2008), 75.

2. See also Isaiah 58:6–7.

3. See also Jeremiah 22:3.

4. For this section one can consult Chapters 3–4 of Matthew Soerens and Jenny Hwang, *Welcoming the Stranger: Justice, Compassion and Truth in the Immigration Debate* (Downers Grove, IL: IVP Press, 2009). Much of my summary reflects their fine discussion of this question.

5. The Immigration Act of 1924 (The Johnson-Reed Act), U.S Department of State Office of the Historian; Robert K. Murray, *The 103rd Ballot: Democrats and the Disaster in Madison Square Garden* (New York: Harper & Row, 1976), 7.

6. There is so much more to consider here that space does not allow. For example, in a kind of irony our laws have helped to generate and as a way to show some desire to honor the law, many undocumented aliens obtain false Social Security cards and pay into our system, even though they know they can never recover, under current conditions, that money. Would it not be better to clean all this up? For more detail on how the system works and the ways and restrictions of gaining one's way in, see chapter 4 of Soerens and Hwang, *Welcoming the Stranger*. There also is the current policy of "aging out" that reflects where things stood as of May 2014. James Barron of the *New York Times* describes aging out this way: "Under federal law, immigrants can name children under 21 as dependents on their applications. But unless the parents receive green cards before the children turn 21, the children 'age out' of the immigration system. So they [the children] face a painful choice as they approach adulthood: remain here illegally or return to countries they left years ago." Some immigrant parents upon arrival were invited to help schools with students who shared their language. These immigrant teachers were put in the visa

line upon arrival, but the process has now taken so long that their children are also at risk, even though the children were raised here and are culturally more American. All of this is so different than the Ellis Island hours of the past and the experience of people who simply came here and faithfully carried out the tasks they were brought here to perform. For the story that ended up before the Supreme Court, see James Barron, "Justices May Hold Fate of Children Who Lost Their Place in Immigration Line," http://www.nytimes.com/2014/05/19/nyregion/justices-may-hold-fate -of-children-who-lost-place-in-immigration-line.html?hp.

7. This last section is the argument against James K. Hoffmeier, *The Immigration Crisis: Immigrants, Aliens, and the Bible* (Wheaton, IL: Crossway, 2009), 146, which claims nothing about the situation requires changing current law. Technically he is right. One can continue as is. No change is required. The question is whether this is the moral and right thing to do in light of the shifts and inequities that have only been surveyed and the dysfunction many on all sides do sense exists. When he goes on to argue for a form of humane expatriation (deportation), then myriads of issues tied to the breakup of families are left undeveloped. Nevertheless, his concern for honoring the law in some way is a part of the discussion. Finally, Hoffmeier's claim that the foreigner in the OT is limited to those who obtained permission to be in the nation overstretches the biblical meaning, almost viewing the ancient world like the modern one in terms of how nations operated and people traveled. It also ignores the ethical core example from Jesus of the Good Samaritan and the OT rationale for leaving part of one's field unharvested. There is no "residency" test for that passage and no limit to the neighbor or who the foreigner might be. It can be anyone who passes by and needs access to that corner of the field. The Samaritan, a foreigner traveling in Israel in the parable, cares for one who is a foreigner to him.

8. For details, Frederica Marsi, "Syrian Refugees Overwhelm Lebanon to the Breaking Point," *USA Today*. November 19, 2015 (http://www.usa today.com/story/news/world/2015/11/19/lebanon-beirut-refugees-syria /73475896).

9. Of course if this were consistently applied with full sanctions of deportation no one would be left, but the damage to families split would be done. So it is not clear how sequencing really is a genuine sequence.

CHAPTER 7—GUN CONTROL:
SELF-DEFENSE OR RESTRAINT?

Philip J. Cook and Kristin A. Goss, *The Gun Debate: What Everyone Needs to Know* (New York: Oxford University Press, 2014), 214.

1. Cook and Goss, *The Gun Debate*. John R. Lott, Jr., *More Guns, Less Crime: Understanding Crime and Gun Control Laws* (Chicago: University of Chicago Press, 2010), 1, placed the number at 270 million in 2010.

2. http://www.cfr.org/society-and-culture/us-gun-policy-global-compari sons/p29735.

3. Another work going in the same direction is Glenn Beck, *Control: Exposing the Truth about Guns* (New York: Threshold Editions 2013).

4. Craig Whitney, *Living with Guns: A Liberal's Case for the Second Amendment* (New York: PublicAffairs, 2012), 154. He also cites the example of Chicago, which with strict guns laws put into effect still has a rising gun murder rate.

5. Sabrina Tavernise, "In Missouri, Fewer Gun Restrictions and More Gun Killings," *New York Times*, December 22, 2015 (http://www.nytimes.com /2015/12/22/health/in-missouri-fewer-gun-restrictions-and-more-gun -killings.html).

6. Ibid., 211.

7. Some argue that any governmental gun lists risk undercutting the original intent of the amendment, to allow protection from a corrupt government. This might be correct, but the question is whether this risk is greater than the public good of having a system that prevents one who might abuse the right from having guns. It would seem some level of trust in our society must be present for laws to have any value at all. The fear this concern expresses seems excessive in a country where citizens do possess ultimate political authority.

8. The list here mostly follows Whitney's suggestions in *Living with Guns*, 215–50.

9. For a study suggesting proposals in this area from the Consortium for Risk-Based Firearm Policy, entitled *Guns, Public Health, and Mental*

Illness: An Evidence-Based Approach for Federal Policy, see http://www
.jhsph.edu/research/centers-and-institutes/johns-hopkins-center-for
-gun-policy-and-research/publications/GPHMI-Federal.pdf.

10. Another shooting in Aurora, Colorado, involved a person whose psychologist knew he was a threat to the public.

11. Whitney, *Living with Guns,* 224.

12. http://smartgunlaws.org/straw-purchases-policy-summary/.

CHAPTER 8—FOREIGN POLICY AND GLOBALIZATION: NATIONAL INTEREST OR COMMON GOOD?

Charles A. Kupchan, *No One's World: The West, The Rising Rest, and the Coming Global Turn* (Oxford: Oxford University Press, 2012), 9.

Paul Collier, *The Bottom Billion: Why the Poorest Countries Are Failing and What Can Be Done about It* (Oxford, UK: Oxford University Press, 2008), xi–xii.

1. Dani Rodrik, *The Globalization Paradox: Democracy and the Future of the World Economy* (New York: W. W. Norton & Co., 2011), xviii–xix.

2. This point is vividly portrayed by Gary Haugen and Victor Boutros in *The Locust Effect: Why the End of Poverty Requires the End of Violence* (New York: Oxford University Press, 2014). The authors' work with the International Justice Mission shows how deep the problems are. Here is one quotation from their introduction: "When we think of global poverty we readily think of hunger, disease, homelessness, illiteracy, dirty water, and a lack of education, but very few of us immediately think of the global poor's chronic vulnerability to violence—the massive epidemic of sexual violence, forced labor, illegal detention, land theft, assault, police abuse, and oppression that lies hidden underneath the more visible deprivations of the poor."

CHAPTER 9—WAR AND PEACE:
"JUST WAR" OR PACIFISM?

Joseph S. Nye, Jr., *The Future of Power* (New York: PublicAffairs, 2011), 39.

1. Thomas C. Forhlich and Alexander Kent, "Countries Spending the Most on Military," *USA TODAY*, July 12, 2014 (http://www.usatoday.com /story/money/business/2014/07/12/countries-spending-most-on-mili tary/12491639/).

2. See the specific numbers at http://www.usgovernmentspending.com /federal_budget_detail_fy12bs12011n.

3. Matthew has Jesus give his ethical sermon on a mount, while Luke describes it as being on a plain. Parts of Galilee have what we might call hills that level out at the top. Thus we use the designation Sermon on the Mount/Plain. The location of the teaching comes in the same equivalent spot in each gospel, making it likely to be the same event. It is also important to recall that Jesus was an itinerant preacher, so it is possible each gospel writer is simply presenting his sample of Jesus' ethical message.

4. This pacifist position has been argued for by John Yoder, *The Politics of Jesus* (Grand Rapids, MI: Eerdmans, 1994).

5. John Yoder, *Nevertheless: The Varieties and Shortcomings of Religious Pacifism*, 2nd ed. (Scottsdale, PA: Herald, 1992) goes through twenty-one ways pacifism is presented.

6. A full discussion of this approach can be found in J. Daryl Charles and Tim J. Demy, *War, Peace and Christianity: Questions and Answers from a Just War Perspective* (Wheaton, IL: Crossway, 2010).

7. Ibid., 122–27.

8. A famous defense of letting war be war comes from Carl von Clausewitz, *On War* (1832; English edition, Princeton: Princeton University Press, 1989). A European Prussian general, his work was widely influential and was translated into many languages.

9. Charles and Demy, *War, Peace, and Christianity*, 51–53.

10. For a discussion of how various religious traditions view this question, see the Texas faith blog of the *Dallas Morning News*, September 9, 2008,

http://religionblog.dallasnews.com/2008/09/texas-faith-war-and-faith
.html/.

CHAPTER 10—VIOLENCE AND JUSTICE

Rodney King in an interview during 1992 L.A. riots, https://m.youtube
.com/watch?v=1sONfxPCTU0.

1. Kevin Sack and Megan Thee-Brenan, "Poll Finds Most in U.S. Hold Dim
   View of Race Relations," *New York Times*, July 23, 2015 (www.nytimes
   .com/2015/07/24/us/poll-shows-most-americans-think-race-relations
   -are-bad.html).

2. This question was posed and answered on the Dallas Theological Seminary Podcast known as *The Table*. See Darrell Bock and Tony Evans,
   "Beyond Ferguson: Biblical Racial Reconciliation," April 14, 2015, www
   .dts.edu/thetable/play/biblical-racial-reconciliation. The discussion goes
   from 00:15 to 9:37.

3. This angle was discussed in a second Table podcast with Tony Evans,
   April 21, 2015 (http://www.dts.edu/thetable/play/racial-reconciliation
   -and-church). This discussion goes from 13:38 to 25:36.

CHAPTER 11—EDUCATION:
RELATING TO A GLOBALIZED WORLD

1. Tony Wagner, *The Global Achievement Gap: Why Even Our Best Schools
   Don't Teach the New Survival Skills Our Children Need—And What We
   Can Do About It* (New York: Basic Books, 2014), xix. These statistics are
   from the Organisation for Economic Co-operation and Development
   in 2003. See http://www.oecd.org/education/skills-beyond-school/educa
   tionataglance2003-home.htm (Table A1.1). All the statistics in this paragraph are from this page in Wagner. These are among the latest years for
   comparative statistics at an extensive international level.

2. David Conley for the Foundation's "Toward a More Comprehensive
   Conception of College Readiness" (https://docs.gatesfoundation.org
   /documents/collegereadinesspaper.pdf). See p. 10. Wagner misstates the
   statistics in his book, saying the study said only one in three were pre-

pared for college. It says one in three enter college, only one in seven get a degree.

3. Derek Thompson, "Education and Wages: The More You Learn, the More You Earn," *Atlantic*, January 24, 2012 (http://www.theatlantic.com /business/archive/2012/01/education-and-wages-the-more-you-learn -the-more-you-earn/251926/).

4. See the OCED study summary in "Education at a Glance 2004" (http:// www.oecd.org/education/skills-beyond-school/337144945.pdf). The figures cover the 2002 school year.

5. Michael B. Sauter and Alexander E. M. Hess, "The Most Educated Countries in the World" (http://www.nbcnews.com/business/business-news /most-educated-countries-world-f1B6065913).

6. The statistics for this paragraph are from Paul Manna and Patrick McGuinn, eds., *Education Governance for the Twenty-First Century: Overcoming the Structural Barriers to School Reform* (Washington, DC: The Brookings Institute, 2013), especially chapter 3. The numbers appear to come from a period covering 2007–8, although the chapter is not clear on this.

7. http://www.tncrimlaw.com/civil_bible/horace_mann.htm.

8. John Henry Newman, *The Idea of the University* (New Haven: Yale University Press, 1996), 64–65.

9. David Conley for the Gates Foundation's "Toward a More Comprehensive Conception of College Readiness" (https://docs.gatesfoundation .org/documents/collegereadinesspaper.pdf). See pp. 12–16.

CHAPTER 12—THE FAMILY: SEXUALITY AND INDIVIDUAL RIGHTS

Stanton L. Jones, and Mark A. Yarhouse, *Homosexuality: The Use of Scientific Research in the Church's Moral Debate* (Downers Grove, IL: IVP Academic, 2000), 153.

1. Jones and Yarhouse, *Homosexuality*, 153–54.

2. http://www.childstats.gov/americaschildren/famsoc2.asp.

3. http://www.childtrends.org/?indicators=births-to-unmarried-women. See more at http://www.childtrends.org/?indicators=births-to-unmarried-women#sthash.5bGBondg.dpuf.

4. http://www.childstats.gov/americaschildren/famsoc2.asp.

5. One of the concerns people have who are sensitive to the presence of same-sex desires and relationships is the view that those who defend heterosexuality do not appreciate how "hardwired" some people are who have same sex desires. The claim is made that this is how God made me, so why should I be limited by that? They might say, "This is natural for me." This is an important claim. Still some observations can be made. First, not everyone is hardwired this way. The actual percentage of people we are discussing in this category is small, somewhere less than 5 percent, perhaps as low as 1 percent. Second, "hardwiring" does not mean one should choose to act on those kinds of inclinations. I note that many people are hardwired to lust or to drink to excess, but that does not mean they should exercise the freedom to act on that inclination or even proclivity to go there. However, third, the fact some are hardwired does mean that not everyone with same-sex inclinations should be seen in the same way. Some have found they are able to change in their orientation; others are not so easily moved from there. Where they are is a genuine reflection of their natural inclinations. For them, other choices still exist. On these options, see Wesley Hill, *Washed and Waiting: Reflections on Christian Faithfulness and Homosexuality* (Grand Rapids, MI: Zondervan, 2010) and Christopher and Angela Yuan, *Out of a Far Country: A Gay Son's Search for God and a Broken Mother's Search for Hope* (Colorado Springs: Waterbrook Press, 2011). To challenge someone to reflect morally on his or her choices is no different here than in many other areas of moral choice, where what I am free or even inclined to do may not be best for me to do.

6. Matthew 5:31–32, Mark 10:2–12, and Luke 16:18 also have Jesus discuss divorce. In Mark 10 and Luke 16, the citation of Jesus gives no exceptions for divorce. All the sayings make the point that a divorce pursued leads in effect to adultery in the new relationship because the original vows, meant to be permanent, are violated. The picture makes a powerful rhetorical point that gives emphasis to the idea that marriage is designed to be permanent and stable. Matthew 5 and 19 allow for one exception, sexual immorality. The term used is broad, for a wide array of

sexual infidelities. Paul also addresses the topic of divorce in 1 Corinthians 7:12–16. Paul indicates he knows what Jesus taught, and goes on to mention a second exception for divorce, when an unbeliever abandons a believer and seeks a divorce. The fact Paul can make an addition suggests Jesus' words were not read as intending absolutely no divorce.

7. We do not have space to work through all of these texts in detail. Efforts to argue for scriptural openness to same sex marriage come from those who published the "Queen James Bible." Some in a more limited way argue for monogamous same sex marriage only. The Queen James version made claims for an updated and scholarly reading of eight key biblical texts thought to be negative on the topic. I hosted a podcast that walks through these texts one at a time and critiques those claims directly. For that podcast see http://www.dts.edu/thetable/play/queen-james-passages-old-testament/.

8. The following web page summarizes ten distinct studies making this point: http://www.familyfacts.org/briefs/6/benefits-of-family-for-children-and-adults. The summary of the page entitled "Benefits of Family for Children and Parents" reads, "The intact family appears to offer a myriad of benefits for adults and children. The married home tends to provide a safer and healthier home environment. On average, children in intact families fare better in school, exhibit fewer behavioral problems, and are more likely to form healthy romantic relationships as adults." The following from a 2010 Nicholson Foundation report says much the same thing: "Research indicates that children are more likely to become healthy and productive adults when their families are stable. Poverty, unemployment, and low education levels can diminish parental capacity for consistent and involved parenting. When families experience these life stresses, stable and nurturing relationships necessary for a child's healthy development can be disrupted. Domestic violence, homelessness or inadequate housing, and lack of social supports often overwhelm parents, as can caring for children who are developmentally disabled or who exhibit emotional or behavioral problems. Substance abuse, health problems, and mental illness can also lead to inadequate parenting." (http://www.thenicholsonfoundation-newjersey.org/programs/chi/NicholsonFoundationVulnerableFamilies.pdf).

9. http://researchnews.osu.edu/archive/familystability.htm. A stable home would be one where the child is nurtured and affirmed with parents who

get along reasonably well with each other or a single parent home where there was no divorce previously.

10. http://www.sfsu.edu/news/prsrelea/fy10/001.html.

11. Paul Van de Ven, et al., "A Comparative Demographic and Sexual Profile of Older Homosexually Active Men," *Journal of Sex Research* 34 (1997): 349–60. On p. 354, the modal range of partners was 101–500.

12. http://www.aidsmap.com/Consistent-decline-in-partner-numbers-in -US.-gay-men-in-last-decade-but-no-change-in-condom-use/page /2635086/#item2635089.

13. It should be said that the same kinds of concerns would apply to heterosexual marriages where there is the existence of multiple partners operating in the background. This is why biblical values stress the importance of marital fidelity and speak regularly against adultery and immorality when it comes to sexual relations and marriage.

14. Laws in Utah were pursued with both LGBT and Mormon officials finding agreement and offering forms of mutual legal protection. These laws may not be perfect, but they do show the possibilities of what might be mutually worked out. For a look at the Utah laws, see Sarah Eekhoff Zylstra, "Revisiting Evangelicals' Favorite Same-Sex Marriage Laws," *Christianity Today*, March 27, 2015 (http://www.christianitytoday.com /gleanings/2015/march/revisiting-evangelicals-same-sex-marriage-laws -indiana-utah.html). For a discussion of how to look at such pluralism, see John Inazu, "Pluralism Doesn't Mean Relativism," *Christianity Today*, April 6, 2015 (web only: http://www.christianitytoday.com/ct/2015 /april-web-only/pluralism-doesnt-mean-relativism.html).

CHAPTER 13—ABORTION AND EMBRYOS: RIGHT TO LIFE OR RIGHT TO CHOOSE?

Robert D. George and Christopher Tollefsen, *Embryo: A Defense of Human Life*, 2nd ed. (Princeton, NJ: Witherspoon Institute, 2011), 18.

1. Bernard Nathanson, *The Hand of God: The Journey from Life to Death by the Abortion Doctor Who Changed His Mind* (Washington, DC: Regnery Publishers, 2001), and Bernard Nathanson with Richard Ostling, *Aborting America* (Toronto: Life Cycle Books, 1979).

2. Christopher Kaczor, *The Ethics of Abortion: Women's Rights, Human Life, and the Question of Justice* (New York: Routledge, 2011).

3. For discussion of these verses, see M. G. Kline, "*Lex Talionis* and the Human Fetus," *Journal of the Evangelical Theological Society* 20 (1977): 193–201; W. House, "Miscarriage or Premature Birth: Additional Thoughts on Exodus 21:22–25," *Westminster Theological Journal* 41 (1978): 108–23; S. E. Loewenstamm, "Exodus XXI 22–25," *Vetus Testamentum* 27 (1977): 352–60.

4. For this discussion and a walk through the options, see Maureen L. Condic, *When Does Human Life Begin?: A Scientific Perspective.* Westchester Institute White Paper Series, Volume 1, Number 1 (Thornwood, NY: The Westchester Institute for Ethics and the Human Person, 2008). Available over the Net at: http://bdfund.org/wordpress/wp-content/uploads /2012/06/wi_whitepaper_life_print.pdf. See especially pp. 1–2 and notes 4–10. Gastrulation is when the embryo moves from a singular layer to a three-layered structure. Dr. Condic is an associate professor of Neurobiology and Anatomy at the University of Utah School of Medicine, with an adjunct appointment in the Department of Pediatrics. She received her undergraduate degree from the University of Chicago and her doctorate from the University of California at Berkeley.

5. Condic, *When Does Human Life Begin?*, pp. 11–12. She also points out that unlike, say, an automobile that comes off an assembly line complete, the ability of an embryo to manage life continues in replication as long as there is life. If I may coin an analogy with marriage vows, it continues "till death does its part." A parallel and more detailed scientific description of this process can be found in George and Tollefsen, *Embryo*, 36–41.

6. Georgia Hageman, "My Life as a Pregnant Teenager," *New Zealand Herald*, June 28, 2014 (http://www.nzherald.co.nz/lifestyle/news/article.cfm ?c_id=6&objectid=11283247). When this article was published, some criticized the publication of this opinion piece, saying it glorified teen pregnancy. It does not. This young lady assessed her situation, faced up to her actions, and took responsibility for them. She had a proper, mature response to a poor previous choice, wrote about it, and sought to encourage others in the same situation to consider their choices.

7. Some might and do raise the issue of cases of rape, but the trauma tied to this act often precludes conception. When conception does occur, the option of adoption does remain. Admittedly this is a discussable case where people might differ in their resolution. However the bulk of the circumstances involving abortion do not touch either the example of a mother's health being at risk or rape. Most abortions do not have near the moral ambiguity of these two situations.

CONCLUSION: ENGAGEMENT, RESPECT, AND LOVING YOUR NEIGHBOR

1. http://money.cnn.com/interactive/pf/taxes/top-income-tax-rate/?iid =EL. Sort by tax rate.

2. Other countries with higher rates were: Belgium (54 percent), the Netherlands (52 percent), Spain (52 percent), France (51 percent), Finland (49 percent), Greece (49 percent), Portugal (49 percent), Italy (49 percent), Ireland (48 percent), Germany (48 percent), and Iceland (46 percent).

3. http://money.cnn.com/interactive/pf/taxes/top-income-tax-rate/?iid =EL. Sort by income.

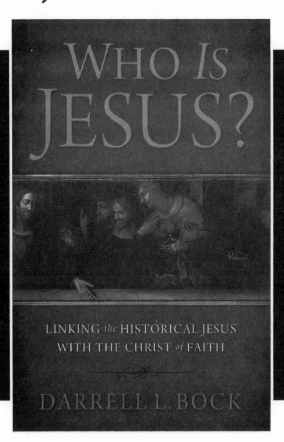